PRAISE FOR
THE HUMAN V

'Having worked for many big-hearted and thoughtful companies, from Levi's to Gap and now Airbnb, I know that an intentional, authentic and democratized approach to creating a human-centric workplace is a recipe for success. The principles set out in *The Human Workplace* are helpful for any company that emphasizes purpose and identity, connection with the company, each other and the community, as well as co-creation and two-way dialogue with employees. This is a helpful guide on how to grow by design.' **Mark Levy, Airbnb's first Head of Employee Experience**

'The future of work is going to be very different from what we know and are comfortable with. The unpredictable nature of that future makes it enticing to leap for the nearest apparent solution, to adopt the latest fad organizational model, to spend millions on technology, or to copy the "best practices" of the shiny-new-flavour-of-the-month startup. Andy Swann knows better than most that things just aren't that straightforward. Bringing his work at the coalface of organizational change with him, he leads us through the challenges, debunks the fads and offers practical and effective ways of not only coping with the challenges of the future but possibly even enjoying them.' **Euan Semple, author, speaker and Business Strategist**

'There is so much simplistic theory around, but often talk of culture and workplace misses the human element (even when it claims not to). Humans doing good stuff is what counts, and this isn't separate from culture, yet so often seems to be described as such. This book is pragmatic, relevant, current – it should be required reading for all leaders claiming "People are the most important thing to me" and selectively pointing at other companies saying "I want that one" without understanding the elements, ie, people.' **Andy Meikle, former Chief People Officer, JustGiving, and Founder, Folk Consulting**

'*The Human Workplace* offers a thoughtful and incisive examination of our complicated relationship with our work, its meaning and our attitudes. In this comprehensively researched book, Andy Swann considers the full scope of how we work, from the interpersonal to the networks and communities on which we rely, and how this is translating into today's society. In an age of digitization and artificial intelligence, Swann repeatedly finds that applying our shared humanity is the most important element of a high-performing workplace. From case studies to personal reflections, he explores engaging workplace comparisons and finds ingenuity at work in work. This book made me reconsider how we should shape the future of work and appreciate that it will be those who are constantly learning in our high-speed world that will deserve success for their teams and a resilient future for their organizations.' **Tim Pointer, former HR Director, Dixons Carphone, and Founder, Starboard Thinking**

The Human Workplace

People-centred organizational development

Andy Swann

KoganPage

First published in Great Britain and the United States in 2018 by Kogan Page Limited

2nd Floor, 45 Gee Street	c/o Martin P Hill Consulting	4737/23 Ansari Road
London	122 W 27th St, 10th Floor	Daryaganj
EC1V 3RS	New York, NY 10001	New Delhi 110002
United Kingdom	USA	India

www.koganpage.com

© Andy Swann, 2018

The right of Andy Swann to be identified as the author of this work has been asserted by him in accordance with the Copyright, Designs and Patents Act 1988.

ISBN   978 0 7494 8122 3
E-ISBN   978 0 7494 8123 0

British Library Cataloguing-in-Publication Data

A CIP record for this book is available from the British Library.

Library of Congress Cataloging-in-Publication Data

Names: Swann, Andy, author.
Title: The human workplace : people-centred organizational development/Andy
    Swann.
Description: 1st Edition. | New York: Kogan Page Ltd, [2017] | Includes
    bibliographical references and index.
Identifiers: LCCN 2017035673 (print) | LCCN 2017032402 (ebook) | ISBN
    9780749481230 (ebook) | ISBN 9780749481223 (alk. paper)
Subjects: LCSH: Corporate culture. | Work environment.
Classification: LCC HD58.7 (print) | LCC HD58.7 .S952 2017 (ebook) | DDC
    658.3/12–dc23

Typeset by Integra Software Services Pvt. Ltd., Pondicherry
Print production managed by Jellyfish
Printed and bound by CPI Group (UK) Ltd, Croydon, CR0 4YY

References to websites (URLs) were accurate at the time of writing. Neither the author(s) nor Kogan Page is responsible for URLs that may have expired or changed since the manuscript was prepared.

CONTENTS

ACKNOWLEDGEMENTS

Thanks to everyone involved in contributing to this book. Not least the amazing innovators, practitioners, thinkers and doers who gave time, energy, conversation and insight. Your names are all given pride of place next to your contributions throughout the book! Thanks also to the amazing people who helped arrange and facilitate conversations and interviews, particularly Shweta Agarwal, Sébastien Barangé and Émilie Proulx. Your help has been invaluable.

Somehow it got there and a huge thanks needs to go to everyone at Kogan Page, particularly Sophia Levine for your unerring patience as the project grew and grew! Thanks also to Lucy Carter for thinking of me in the first place.

People who, although maybe not credited by name in the book, contributed through conversation and inspiration include Doug Shaw, Alison Germain, Mark Catchlove, everyone involved in All About People 2016, Simon White, Matt Desmier, the entire team at BDG architecture + design and all the others who I may have missed! Rich Lloyd, I think you already know how much the daily check-ins and moral support helped me through the process. A huge thanks to Nicole Antonio-Gadsdon and John Baldino for reviewing chapters on the way. And Sasha, just as I was writing the conclusion, you sent a link that inspired it ... perfect timing!

I should have started with my family, but it's hard to express what this project, alongside my incessant work-adventuring has put them through! All of you have been amazing throughout. I don't deserve to have you around me and I know these words don't do any of it justice.

There were some beautiful moments of synergy during the process and if it went on any longer, there would be more. Just as our organizations are, this will always be a work in progress. It's a case of knowing when to step back!

Most importantly, thanks to you for reading *The Human Workplace*.

Introduction

Why your workplace needs to be human

The modern world and old organizations are not compatible.

Right now, we're communicating, thinking, collaborating, sharing, working and playing in ways that couldn't have been imagined two decades ago, yet somehow many of our businesses and the structures employed to operate them remain the same, carrying on in the way they always have. There are many reasons why this is completely unsustainable and we're going to explore these as we journey through what makes a human workplace.

The world has changed beyond recognition. Socially, economically, politically and technologically, things are shifting and changing in near instants, often unpredictably. The ever-increasing advances in tech are facilitating these changes and as a result, *normal* is now a fluid thing. These contributing factors are important individually and collectively, we could write full books on each of them. People more qualified than me probably will.

What we're concerned with here is how it's possible to build an organization that not only fits today, but is ready for tomorrow in all its unpredictability, whatever that may bring. I've spent the last few years researching work and organizations first-hand, trying to understand the way they work, why they do things the way they do and how they could be better.

One key discovery I've made is that, regardless of the size, scale, sector, industry or complexity of an organization, there are clear things it can do to create success in changeable times. In fact, even some of the most complex global organizations are doing incredible things, despite being confined by very outdated structures. In this book alone, we will discover initiatives and examples from Microsoft, LEGO, Coca-Cola, Schneider Electric, CGI and many others. Between them, the organizations that provide our case studies employ over a million people globally. They are just the tip of the iceberg. The clear message is that building an organization around people is not only possible, but achievable for everyone.

There's a general will for change from both the top and bottom of the triangle. The biggest blocker seems to be the restrictive control the typical organizational model places on its people. Knowledge, ideas, experience, creativity, care, consideration and perspective are embedded in every single person not only employed by, but interacting with our organizations. Plugging into this is essential if the organization is to be as adaptable and responsive as it needs to be, so the power for creating the future is always embedded in the organization's community, not sitting in its boardroom.

Although the will to unlock the future by unleashing people is perhaps not yet as coherent or universal as it can (or needs to) be, it's exciting to know that the same factors that can be leveraged to drive change are enabling people at all levels within these sometimes complex structures, to take responsibility for creating change where they see a need for it in the interests of the organization. We no longer have to wait for permission – to some extent mischief is saving our businesses.

It all sounds very counter-intuitive. Surely there is a model to implement that will tell us how to create success for the future? That's just the thing – there's not. There is no blueprint for designing a people-first organization. To understand why, we need to start rethinking what an organization is, why it exists and how it works – we need to place it in the context of the world in which it operates.

Every organization is a unique collection of people, doing something unique, with a unique mission. So to truly thrive, it needs to embrace what it is that makes it great – its people. Doing this enables organizations to flex and adapt in any way the world requires. Unleashing people unleashes the tools for success. It's a simple mechanism.

Put simply, when people thrive, organizations thrive too. The future of work is all about people.

Making this real is 99 per cent common sense. Some of the most amazing brands, successful companies and complex corporations are leaping forward in this area. It's the sum of these things, implemented in a way that suits each individual organization, that creates success. Far from being more complicated, this is all about removing complexity and creating simpler organizations.

Outside the workplace we know that if you treat people well, they will treat you well and that's the essence of all this. As we work through this alternative perspective on organizations, we'll explore very real actions you can take that will create positive impact in your organization. It doesn't matter whether you're a CEO or a cleaner, three people in a garage or a global team of 100,000 people. This stuff works.

We live in the age of ideas. New is happening already. It's just a question of keeping up.

Forget behaving like a startup!

There's a lot of talk around organizations behaving like startups and it's a conversation I hear in everything from culture development to physical workplace design. This is a reaction to traits that newsworthy startups show and is misguided. What we really need is for our organizations to behave like people.

The startup comparison frames the traditional mechanics of business in a new way. It's advantageous in that it grasps the successes of the most effective startups where they show how fewer people in less formal circumstances can create real global impact with fewer resources and apparently less effort. This is great, but it only accounts for the startups we hear about and the ones we hear about are those that are newsworthy.

The startup conversation

So many organizations are starting to investigate how they can capture the essence of the startup mentality and unleash it in their own business. There are many definitions of what that essence actually is, but here's a summary of findings from my work actually asking complex organizations – *what is a startup?*

1 *Startup traits*
   A newly established, fast moving, energetic business with big ideas and the ability to adapt and implement them quickly.
2 *Typical environments*
   Collaborative, connected communities that move quickly and focus on what's important at that time, within the context of their overall aim.
3 *Examples of high-impact startups*
   Instagram, Snapchat, YouTube in its day. All examples of how a close-knit community with a big idea can create impact and define the future.

It's nothing specific, rather a mentality and approach to organizing. In reality, more established organizations have the advantage of definition and direction, they just need to get out of the way and allow this more dynamic mindset to emerge.

For every amazing startup doing amazing things, there is an amazing established business doing equally amazing things, but these things may be buried within its traditional structure. There's a romantic vision of 'sticking it to the man' that persists and makes it newsworthy when underdogs achieve great things. A small product innovation project at Coca-Cola could create category impacts of over $100m, change global consumer habits and receive zero press coverage, yet startup Jimmy's Iced Coffee achieving projected £2m turnover in 2015–16 received national news coverage via *The Daily Telegraph* (Telegraph.co.uk, 2015).

It's a lovely dream that the secrets to success lie in our garages and that if we can just get corporate workers into hoodies, every problem will be solved. It's a crazy truth that in some ways this is possible through adopting different mindsets, although we shouldn't focus solely on the idea that the answer lies in the format of the startups themselves.

What they offer is a lack of formality and a connection where people congregate around a shared belief or goal – something they really believe in. Because they build things they really want to use themselves, the team are the first customers and most passionate advocates. There's an energy and dynamism that comes with the agility of a small team. They learn as they go, pivoting to adapt to the market, because there is no major marketing or advertising budget to attempt to attract the market by brute force. The only brute force in a successful startup is the will to succeed.

These are the best startups though. Estimates are that 90 per cent of startup companies fail (Fortune.com, 2014) – and that's just the ones that are registered, or surface in some way. How many don't we hear about that fall by the wayside before they even get on the map?

The secret isn't behaving like a startup, or even the successful 10 per cent of startups. The traits those organizations have are the same as the traits of amazing established organizations, without the dilution or structure around them. It's a connection between brand, business, organization and people. It's the ability to flex and respond, plugging in to the two-way exchange of information and ideas to create a platform for mutual success.

When running internal workshops for a leading creative company in the United Kingdom, I asked the participants to brainstorm traits of startups. These were the top three: 1) energy; 2) direction/mission; and 3) passion.

You don't have to be a startup to achieve these things in your organization!

In an exploration exercise with the entire team of an established creative agency, I posed a question to the participants: *How can your organization behave more like a startup?* One of the common responses was: *Why would we want to?*

It's essential not to get blinded by the aesthetics of successful startups and really understand what it is about those organizations we may be envious of and want to aspire to. Existing organizations have history, hard work and a story behind them – all the things startups are actually aspiring to. If the goal is to connect with people, that counts as a head start.

The human workplace is one that adapts, innovates fast, involves everyone, communicates, understands and acts in perpetuity. It creates relationships rather than transactions.

People are emotional, responsive, individual. That's what our organizations need to be, creating a story and telling it in their own way.

What a human workplace is

The idea of a human workplace has no fixed definition. It manifests in different ways. Because there is no end game, just progress in an ever-changing world, it's impossible to define an end point. A human workplace is one that develops itself people-first, realizing that it's the connection with people that drives it forward. As a result, we all have our own definition of what that should look like.

Generally, a human workplace could be defined as:

- committed to enabling performance through people;
- having a clear mission;
- focused on long-term development through creativity and innovation;
- sensitive to the benefits of connection and wellness;
- collaborative, communicative and open;
- non-linear.

We'll discover examples of organizations demonstrating all of these traits, not necessarily all at once. As I had conversations with influencers and activists for this book, I discovered that asking the question '*What makes a human organization?*' elicited a different response every time, based on perception, context, organization and personal preference. So even if this list is a good starting point, it's essential to remember that when we each set the questions our organization needs to answer, we necessarily create an individual answer too!

Whether you term it as an organization that puts its people first and focuses on collective achievement through a quality employee experience, one that operates a flatter, democratized structure or one that behaves as a whole in the way a living, breathing human would, your definition is valid – because it's yours. We spend far too much time on models and rules, formality and over-seriousness in the world of work, all of which hinder progress towards what we're really trying to achieve.

For me, the human workplace is a simpler, better way of designing your organization so it's optimized for both today and tomorrow. There's no point trying to predict the future, just as there's no point trying to hang onto a fading past. All we should be concerned with is creating the best platform for success that is ready for anything the world may throw at it.

Defining your human workplace

Your definition of a *human workplace* is unique. It needs to be, because it's the combination of:

- your business's purpose;
- the behaviours it wants to drive;
- what it stands for;
- the organizational platform it creates to allow its people to thrive.

Every human workplace is a constantly evolving work in progress, designed to enable people to do their best work in pursuit of the business goals. Because of that, it's designed people-first, viewing them as the end users and providing them with the optimum experience.
   We'll build your definition throughout the book.

Little over a decade ago, Blackberry handsets with Gameboy-esque LCD screens were revolutionizing the way we worked. E-mail on the go created the always-on worker. Even today, many organizations are yet to understand fully how to adapt and create policies that cater for the always-on worker without over-working them. Despite the lasting effects of its initial impact, in 2016 the company announced it would no longer be making Blackberry phones (*The Guardian*, 2016). Only 14 years after starting, taking the world by storm and fundamentally changing the way we work, the Blackberry phone is dead, rendered obsolete by smartphone technology that innovated more quickly and in a way that people actually wanted.

Blackberry was unable to retain a connection to the community it created, too slow to innovate and as a result it lost them. A human organization is predisposed to keeping connections alive and moves quickly enough to stay relevant. Being a human workplace is not about being a specific size or shape, it's about behaviour and acceptance of individuality.

All fully human organizations should be:

- clear in their identity;

- genuinely connected with people (customers and employees);

- positive promoters of two-way communication.

We're going to look at many examples of how organizations of all shapes and sizes are doing amazing things to build success around people. Some of the most innovative practitioners from the most exciting organizations will be sharing their thoughts and experiences with us. Most importantly though, I'll be offering you simple questions to ask your organization and actions you can take to drive your organization to a more successful future, whether you're the cleaner or the CEO.

The Human Workplace is not a specific blueprint. It's a set of ideas for you to work into your own story. Some of the things we'll see are in evidence in even the most complex organizations and the entire conversation is designed to help you create answers to the challenges your organization faces in the world today.

I think I'm yet to experience the ultimate human organization, but I've seen many, many great things. Things any organization can learn from, that nine times in ten not only increase performance now, they also improve the experience for everyone involved.

This book is about exploration. It's up to you to create your definition of a human workplace in the context of your own organization. Design it and build it to be as individual as the people it contains. It's the only way.

Why you need this book

Whatever we do, wherever we sit in our organization, everything is changing around us. If you're unable to step back, make sense of it and create your place in it, you don't fit. If you don't fit, you're obsolete and if you're obsolete ... you get the picture.

The Human Workplace is written to help you step back, consider your organization and reframe your perspective. It will help you understand what's really important and what's just noise, fill you with ideas, but most importantly inspire you to action. Ideas are great – they're a huge commodity today, but if you do nothing about them they may as well not exist. As everyone's grandmother said to them at some point:

Actions speak louder than words.

Everyone around you is acting. Stake your claim for the future here!

This new world of work, workplace and organizations operates in a very different way to the suited and booted hierarchical view of business we're still taught at school. The old ways are being attacked from every angle and for good reason. The work we do and the way we do it, how our businesses operate and how they find their place in the world sits in the middle of the swirling change we see all around us. Education, the political landscape, technology, the economy – all are shifting and as a result the way it's always been no longer cuts it for our organizations. Even if they want to, they can't infinitely continue to operate the way they once did.

CASE STUDY

By the year 2000, the retailer Tesco had a presence in every single UK postal code, except one. Through decades of aggressive growth, it owned a huge part of the market just by being the de facto place to shop. A no-frills approach offered reasonably low prices, a basic customer experience and a very standard transactional employee experience.

Just over a decade later and the landscape had changed dramatically, catching Tesco flat-footed. People suddenly had choice. Online shopping brought other retailers to the door of the consumer and discount chains left Tesco with no appeal to its shoppers. Equally, the people working at Tesco were there for a job, not because they wanted to be and that amplified the situation further. By 2016, the relationship between employer and employee was damaged to the extent that Tesco launched a campaign to encourage managers to use basic courtesies in their dealings with staff (*The Guardian*, 2016)!

Previously people went to Tesco because they had to, not because they wanted to. Once they no longer had to, they stopped going and the retailer found itself in serious and well-documented financial trouble (BBC, 2015). Tesco's response was not in creating improved connections with people, but through cutting prices in a war they could never win.

Propped up by sell-offs and a cash pool it has the luxury of time to realize that the only way it will succeed into the future is through creating a real connection with people.

Without the ability to buy time, many smaller (and some larger) organizations have failed and continue to fail. It's simple to avoid this, yet why do they fail to do so? Because our organizations are built to be rigid, slow and unresponsive. They are pre-programmed systems, not living, breathing, human workplaces that reflect and connect with the people that align with them.

When trying to adapt and change, organizations naturally look for theory. They search for a model or blueprint that can be implemented step-by-step to provide the future success. It won't work!

It's not easy to be an organization in this crazy new world where Google can arise from someone's garage, yet 10 years later be acting like the biggest corporate giants, while recent graduates can create Instagram and grow it to billion dollar valuations at the same time Kodak flaps wildly to save itself. The rules have been completely rewritten.

The obvious answer for those with money is to spend it. Hence the misguided investment in systems and models that may or may not work. Holacracy – one of the more popular self-management models – is a prime example of an 'alternative' approach to organizational structure that is just as complicated as the system it tries to replace and comes with just as many drawbacks.

Whether you're building an organization from scratch, or developing an existing one of any size, the first thing to realize is that it's individual. You can't please all of the people all of the time, but you can create a connection with the right people, both customers and workers and create the platform for them to thrive, which allows your organization to thrive as a result.

As the combination of the sum of its parts, your organization is completely unique. So while aspects of models, theories and ideas will be useful to you, the only real answer is your own. One you create just for your organization. That's the fundamental thing this book will help you realize.

The very real truth about organizational development is this:

- Most people are not your audience. They will never come and work with you or purchase from you, because you don't have a connection with them and can't reach them.

- If people aren't connected with you through some common bond, no matter how hard or artificially you try to force that connection, it will never last and will only harm your organization in the long run.

- If you lose the connection at any point from first contact onwards, you'll become invisible. Worse still, people may talk negatively about you.

- If people hear what you have to say but choose not to align with you, move on. They aren't your people.

It's an identity thing. Just as part of being human starts with being an individual and having an identity, the same can be said for the best organizations in the modern world. I say best, because the idea of *success* is open to perception. For decades we've confused that word with *profit*, but no more. Success is however your organization defines it and that's one of the things we're going to do here.

Again, there is no one size fits all. There is only what is the right fit for your organization and its people. Over the coming pages we're going to redefine your view of your organization, by understanding what it truly means to build your human organization and what happens when you do.

Your views of what constitutes an organization, a workplace, even an employee will be challenged and the examples, ideas and observations will be accompanied by a series of exercises and actions you can take to make immediate impact. My aim is to help you realize that:

- No matter what your position, it's possible to create positive impact within your organization.
- When people thrive, organizations thrive too.
- The way we create, understand and interact with organizations is changing – if they don't respond, trouble will follow.

How to use *The Human Workplace*

The Human Workplace is grouped into sections. Within each section you will find ideas, examples and inputs from leading thinkers and doers. You will also find simple questions and actions that you can work through by yourself or take into your organization. They will help you create change, or perhaps build from scratch.

There is no right or wrong way to work through the book. If you have the time, a cover-to-cover reading, considering the ideas in sequence will give you the best view of everything from a height. I believe this is called a 'helicopter view'. It's the ultimate perspective.

Equally though, if you're short of time or have a specific area you want to focus on in your organization (eg people, physical workplace, activity, innovation or making change), going straight there will be effective for you. Dip in and out, take the bits you need and introduce yourself to a few of the ideas you don't know you need to incorporate yet.

We'll be following this journey through looking at:

- the context our organizations operate in;
- how we structure them;
- connecting people and organizations;
- creating the right environment for people to thrive;
- driving the right actions, innovation and creativity;
- making the change to become a human organization.

Whatever you choose, this book is your platform to create your own experience from. It doesn't matter where you start, it only matters that you do!

Task 1: what is a human organization?

This book is all about building your own interpretation of a Human Workplace and thinking about how your organization could adopt it. Let's start with a few conceptual ideas. There are no wrong or right answers here and your responses can evolve at any time!

How would you define a Human Organization?

What would it feel like to work there?

Three ways that would be different to your current workplace.

Three ideas for things you could do now to help your organization focus on people.

References

Ahmed, K (2015) *Tesco: Where it went wrong*, bbc.co.uk, 19 January. Available from http://www.bbc.com/news/business-30886632 [Accessed 17 April 2017].

Burn-Callander, R (2015) 'Buyers Circle Jimmy's Iced Coffee as Turnover Tops' £2m, *The Daily Telegraph*, 5 October. Available from www.telegraph.co.uk/finance/businessclub/11913144/Buyers-circle-Jimmys-Iced-Coffee-as-turnover-tops-2m.html [Accessed 17 April 2017].

Butler, S (2016) 'Managers Maketh Management: Tesco Bosses told to be Nicer to Staff', *The Guardian*, 16 March. Available from www.theguardian.com/business/2016/mar/16/tesco-managers-polite-new-initiative [Accessed 17 April 2017].

Griffith, E (2014) *Why startups fail, according to their founders*, Fortune, 25 September. Available from http://fortune.com/2014/09/25/why-startups-fail-according-to-their-founders/ [accessed 17 April 2017].

Monaghan, M (2016) 'Blackberry to stop making phones', *The Guardian*, 28 September. Available from www.theguardian.com/technology/2016/sep/28/blackberry-to-stop-making-phones-handsets [Accessed 17 April 2017].

Getting to grips with the basics 01

Every one of us who has ever checked work e-mails on a smartphone at a time we should have been either asleep, or doing something important like playing with our kids, eating a meal, or looking as we cross the road, knows two things: the way we work is changing; and the response to this change in the organizations we work for is way behind.

The new capabilities are not aligned with the old structures. As a result, many organizations find themselves confused – expecting workers to work more, without modifying policy or procedure to untether them.

This chapter explores:

- the context of the world we work in;
- what an organization really is;
- why starting a movement is important;
- how purpose gives meaning to and shapes the way your organization acts.

A relentlessly changing world of work

While technology is rendering old approaches to work obsolete, many businesses are yet to realize that doing things the way they always have is, far from being the safe option, the biggest risk they can take. As long as it remains possible to download a standardized business model, or see a billion blog posts proclaiming the imperative of *digital transformation*, the greater the danger for organizations without the safety blanket of vast cash reserves (the modern equivalent of time) becomes.

The digital transformation is over. We live in an age where digital is the default setting. Anyone who is yet to transform is either obsolete, or on the way there.

Digital by default

A few years ago, my daughter started school. During one of our first school runs in the British countryside, we passed a traditional red telephone box. Once a feature of street corners everywhere and a cornerstone of the communication infrastructure, by now they were becoming rarer and rarer.

As we chatted and pointed out things we saw as we drove, she suddenly looked confused. Turning to me, she asked *Daddy, what's that red thing*?

That's a telephone box, I replied.

The puzzled look on her face made me realize the need to elaborate further. I explained that in the days before mobile phones, people would use telephone boxes to make a call when they were out and needed to speak to someone.

After a moment's pondering silence, the puzzled look on her face turned to one of incredulity.

But Daddy, why didn't they just Skype?

The idea that there is anything left to transform is an anachronism. While many organizations have, with characteristic sluggishness, recently started to respond to the first wave of change in the digital era by introducing agile environments, flexible working policies and the like, the world they operate in continues to move on at an ever-increasing pace.

That telephone box still stands, but today there's not even a telephone in it. Instead it has become a local book exchange.

The real world doesn't need to ponder a digital transformation – it's already the default setting. Technology is enabling us to create, work and think in new ways that render the structures of the industrial age obsolete. Because of the world view those structures were set up to operate in, changing them is a dangerously laborious process.

It doesn't need to be.

Change needs a response

It's not only a question of *if* organizations are set up to respond to these changes, it's a question of *how* they do it and *how fast*. You can't get on a train after it's left the station, and running behind it is both too slow and too exhausting to ever catch up.

CASE STUDY

Despite fire fighting by selling off various parts of its business, HMV Group went into administration in 2013. It had failed to adapt its retail model to suit the shifting landscape. A large stake in online music download store 7 Digital allowed it to set up its own download store later that same year, as it struggled to find a way back to profit. By that time, the music consumption landscape had shifted again to focus on streaming, leaving HMV's attempts to modernize outmoded by the success of Spotify and, latterly, Apple Music. The real digital opportunity had passed.

HMV returned to profit and by 2015, had once again become the UK's largest retailer of physical music (reclaiming this from Amazon). Capitalizing on a new wave of physical music demand, fuelled partly by vinyl which by 2016 had hit a year-on-year increase of 53 per cent (BBC, 2017), HMV restructured its core business to reflect that of Fopp, a keep-it-simple music and media retailer which it had owned for some years. A journey of musical discovery, clever retail tactics, nostalgia and tangibility.

When HMV finally understood what customers wanted from a physical music store, it managed to return to profit. The retailer had to adapt and managed to do so, by the skin of its teeth, by doing what it was good at in a way people wanted it to, not by doing things the way it had always done them.

When Microsoft launched its Zune portable media player in 2006, the consumer market had long been cornered by Apple's iPod and iTunes. It wasn't innovative – it was a response that came too late. Unsurprisingly, it failed.

Waiting for your competitor to launch something, watching how it performs, then trying to go head-to-head by launching something similar just doesn't work today. The product or service life cycle is too short. By the time your first iteration hits the market, your competitor – assuming they have a connection with their audience – will already be innovating and iterating again, based on real feedback from real users.

There is no time to stand still today, so to respond to the changing demands, expectations and capabilities of the working world, our organizations not only need to act relentlessly, but do so at an almost instantaneous rate. In December 2016, a Tesla customer sent a tweet to its CEO Elon Musk, outlining a frustration with people using a particular Supercharger

Station as public parking. Musk responded, promising action. Within six days, Tesla had announced plans to charge an hourly fee to drivers parking in bays beyond the time needed to charge their cars.

That's the kind of speed required. Not only do you need good ideas, but you need to be able to act on them, with directional input from customer feedback, pretty much instantly to stay ahead of the game. Can your organization act that fast, or is the lag time between idea and execution just too long?

Admittedly, in the Tesla case, the rapid action came from the CEO and the question of whether a less senior employee would have been able to create action so quickly is a huge one. To perform at its optimum, every organization needs to be able to act that quickly in any context. To do that it needs the right information available at all times to inform those decisions, without just waving a finger in the air.

A good idea is a good idea, whoever has it, but unless you act on it, the window of opportunity disappears. Structuring your human workplace to allow information and ideas to flow freely, while trusting people by giving them the permission to act in the best interests of the business, is a major part of achieving amazing performance.

To really understand how it's possible, we need to rethink our fundamental views of what organizations really are and how they fit into the world.

A new basic truth

There was a time when some people may have thought the world looked as seen in Figure 1.1.

Figure 1.1   An outdated linear view of everything

From the knowledge and experience they had available to them up to that point, they held the view that it was flat and therefore you could fall off the edge. I have no evidence that anyone actually held that view, but it's a nice anecdote because, of course, today we know that the world looks as we see it in Figure 1.2.

We all use the facts we have available to form a world view at a given time. In this connected age, where – through smartphones – in our own

Figure 1.2   The world as we know it

pockets we carry the ability to plug into a global brain, we have access to facts, factors and opinions in an instant. Today it would seem crazy to argue the case for a flat, linear world (even though some people do!), because we all have the knowledge and experience that tells us the world is round and dynamic.

It turns, is always changing, always moving forward. It evolves in constant cycles. A year is a cycle, a day is a cycle, seasons, weather, climate – they're all cycles.

In light of the evidence we experience every day and the weight of popular opinion, who in their right mind would argue that the world is flat? It seems so obvious to us today!

For decades, centuries even, the story has been the same in business. Business has seen itself as linear, organizations have seen themselves as linear. You start, create a product or service, sell that product or service, do more of that. Keep doing more of that. Add more products/services, sell more of them. Add more people to sell more products/services. Sell each until you can sell no more, then remove it from sale.

It's a linear approach that assumes we're always moving from A to B. Traditional organizational development and product development aim for finished articles, mature, static structures. Because of that, they don't launch a product, service or idea until they see it as being 100 per cent ready, then they launch with a fanfare, and start the process.

This terrible assumption that linear process is in keeping with the modern world also assumes that what works today will work tomorrow. If we do what we've always done, we will win.

But that doesn't work today. The world has changed and so has business.

Forget what you know

If you're going to create a remarkable, human workplace, fit for the future, it's probably good to have a clear idea of what you're actually building. There's absolutely no need to make anything any more complicated than it needs to be. Complexity is merely an opportunity for confusion to arise and it's been over-used for far too long.

Layer after layer of unnecessary complexity has been piled on top of the fundamentals of business and organizational development, to the point where we've lost sight of what's really important. Professional silos, best practices and industry standards are all evidence of this.

I spent a lot of my early career frustrated with bureaucracy and the inability of organizations I worked in and around to think differently. As a result, I embarked on an experimental year exploring the concept of *work* from the workers' perspective. A big part of the project was an exploration of how organizations influence us and why they operate in the way they do.

I'd already come to realize that the largest organizations have become far more complex than they need to be, for reasons that could fill a book in their own right. A great conversation with Alison Germain, organizational development consultant and coach, who at the time was with NBC Universal, shifted my thinking to an entirely new level.

Ali's premise was that organizations don't actually exist – and she's right! It's a simple idea, but completely true. It's also counter-intuitive to the way we have traditionally worked, where the organization has been held as an altar before which we bow down in gratitude for the gracious provision of employment.

Physically, organizations don't exist. They have no mass, therefore there are no set rules on how they should operate. The systems, models and theories that have developed around them are nothing more than conventions and ideas. They are certainly not gospels. The fact that every now and then, an organization arises that breaks the mould completely by operating in a wholly different way proves that.

Whether Airbnb and its committed focus on the experience all people have in their interactions with it, or Buffer and its global workforce that has no physical workplace, being an outlier is an opportunity to be amazing. Because, when you realize that doing the same thing as everyone else will make you the same as them (and no better), the futility of the norm becomes apparent. Things can be and are done differently, because when something doesn't exist, it can be anything you want it to be. Within the basic parameters of the law, we can create whatever we want to. In fact, some people create highly successful organizations outside those parameters (even though I wouldn't necessarily advise it)!

Forget everything you think you know and build a new picture through your own lens. It's the only way to be completely different from everyone else.

What is an organization anyway?

We're all guilty of something. I've even been doing it in this discussion, so far. We lump the idea of a business and an organization together as a single entity. The words have become interchangeable and it's this that has allowed the complexity to creep in. It's unsurprising, as the two things are so intertwined, but it's also time for clarity.

Your *business* is what you do.

Your *organization* is how you do it.

In most cases, the business does exist. It's registered and certified as real, legally. The type of company you are (partnership, limited and so on) is part of that. Your business is reflected by the brands, products and services it creates. It has a reason for existence that drives the creation of those things and also influences how you go about doing that.

The organization, however, is completely of your making. It's the structure you put in place to do the things that help the business reach its aims. Organizations are frameworks of human making.

It's as simple as that!

Ignore the commercial association of the word 'business' and reimagine it as any kind of exchange. This applies everywhere – in all sectors, industries and approaches. Wherever goods or services are provided, this definition applies. Hospitals, governments, non-profits, charities, they all count. The organizations themselves are a manifestation of the strategy and approach required for that business to do what it's aiming to do, as simply and effectively as possible.

The ideas shared in this book can be applied anywhere. Anywhere that work is done can be a human workplace, because you can design it to be. We need to be clear on that from the start.

End users

Both businesses and organizations have end users. This is important because they are subtly different, yet the approaches taken to provide for each set of end users should be similar. Until recently, this wasn't the case.

The end users of a business are its customers, the recipients of the goods or services it creates.

An organization's end users are its workers, the people creating the business. The organization, as a structure for delivering the aims of a business, is by default a provider of services to those people. As recipients of the services an organization provides, workers are also customers, as shown in Figure 1.3.

The realization that employees and workers are end users has helped to change the philosophy of leading organizations and create the movement towards people-first, human workplaces. From well-known established organizations like eBay and Sky, to pace-setters like Vincit – winner of Best workplace in Europe 2016 – rapidly expanding brands like Airbnb or Netflix and startups like Mind Candy and Deliveroo, the view of workers as end users is forming a central part of their organizational design and development.

Customer experience is a notion that has been around for a long time now. The idea that if you provide the best possible experience for your

Figure 1.3   People as end users

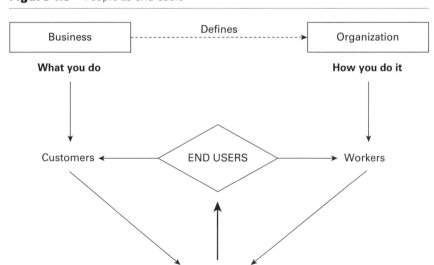

customers, they will not only stay loyal to your business, but act as advocates and evangelists, is today seen as basic common sense. It's exactly the same with the experience you provide to your employees.

Give people a reason to work with you. Give them a reason to stay. Give them a reason to tell the world. Give them the opportunity to do their best work in a way that suits them and is in the best interests of the business. It doesn't sound too hard, does it – so why do we make it so complicated?

Building your amazing human workplace is like building an app, platform or system. If it doesn't meet a need for its end users in a sufficiently accessible way, they won't use it.

Know your end users.

CASE STUDY

Vincit, best workplace in Europe, 2016

'Vincit' is Latin for to conquer or win and the company aims to do just that. With a string of workplace awards over recent years, the software company believes its success comes from a combination of satisfied customers and satisfied employees. This belief that, when people thrive, the organization thrives too, drives a passion for work that has seen Vincit named Best Workplace in Europe 2016.

As director of people operations, Johanna Pystynen takes the lead in creating a workplace where everyone can thrive. She shared with me some of the ideas that drive Vincit forward.

The Vincit philosophy
Everything is based on trust between everyone. If the company trusts people and people trust the company as their employer, we don't need to have so many rules and restrictions. We can allow people to make their own decisions and that leads to success.

When the company was established, the two founders came from big multinationals where they were led by numbers and they both wanted to do something completely different. That's why they decided to build Vincit on trust and create an environment where people can be happy and have the energy to make decisions.

Shifting from control to trust
It's not easy for people to be suddenly given full autonomy. That's why leadership is about creating this environment where you can help people to make their own

decisions. Vincit's leadership style focuses on creating the channels people can use to help them make decisions and have a voice within the organization.

Instead of telling people how to decide or act, or just giving them information, we are trying to develop an environment that helps them to do it on their own.

In this setting, the leader is not the person who has all the information. Across the company we have a lot of experts who know better than the leader. As a leader at Vincit you have to see your role as helping people to succeed; you help them to lead themselves.

Connecting people with organization

We invest a lot of time developing frameworks for our organization. These help people to take responsibility for their own actions by providing the parameters of success. They know what is required, but then have the freedom to choose how to get there and plan the support they need to make it happen.

Both parties need to benefit from the relationship, so when we recruit, as a starting point we make sure people know what environment we offer and whether it can help them to succeed.

Linking the people function to the business

Vincit doesn't actually need a traditional HR function. Our own people team is evolving to become an internal service design team. My mission is to create the kind of human resource function that ensures there are no silos, just an organization that helps all of its people to succeed.

Already, the people team is proactive rather than reactive. We try to avoid risks and help people see the possibilities and threats their own actions may present.

Creating an experience

Most of the time, traditional HR tries to plan things from its own perspective. By building an employee experience, a wider view is required that ties together people functions with other areas like the physical workplace. Already at Vincit we are thinking about welfare through a connection with people.

We have to start with the end users, who are our employees. For example, some of our recruitment processes are developed through a service design approach. Understanding the problems applicants face during the process informs our process. Simple things like responding to every application within 24 hours make an impact on positive experience. The experience starts with a person's first interaction with the organization.

Benefits in traditional terms

Vincit's main business is to sell its competence. When people are happy and motivated, the customer benefits. This is measurable.

We try all the time to help people to know what they want to do next. Our responsibility is to give them projects that automatically help them develop.

As well as the bottom line, when we succeed in these things, we don't have the traditional HR problems other organizations face. People are not feeling stressed or demotivated because their daily worklife is supporting them.

What makes an amazing workplace

People always ask us, 'Don't you have any problems in your company?' I always tell them that we have a lot. The main thing that is different here is that we talk about these problems.

Our people can say openly when they have ideas, criticisms or changes they want to suggest. We take time to listen to them and then do something about it. That's why people feel they have autonomy and they can help us to create a better environment all the time.

Communication is a priority. Coming back to leaders, there's a level of openness required that is difficult for many. It helps the organization for people to know that leaders don't have all the answers, as it starts a conversation that helps progress.

Staying amazing

Vincit's strategy is to stay adaptable. We don't know what happens next, we're just trying to stay agile, so we can see all the possibilities around us. If we succeed in that, we will always have opportunity.

Where to start to become a more people-focused workplace

- Give people autonomy
  People have a lot of thoughts about their own job and are best placed to achieve goals in their own way.

- Provide a framework
  Understanding what they are aiming for helps people to decide how to act.

- Create an open forum
  Make sure there's a place to discuss everything. Vincit uses Slack – every employee is on the same channel and all questions, ideas or issues can open conversation for everyone.

A caveat

Much conversation around organizations and workplaces talks about offices. It's far easier to rethink the way service workers operate than, for example, manufacturing teams or paramedics, due to the increased level of basic, unmovable parameters that exist around their work.

When we're talking about human workplaces, what we're really looking at is how any organization, in any sector, of any size, can build itself around its one constant feature –people – to succeed in the modern world.

The ideas in this book can be applied to any organization, doing anything, anywhere.

Dynamic systems

Socio-economically, the bribe of a career path and a job for life can no longer be guaranteed. Politically, no one knows what will happen next and we're now starting to expect the unexpected as standard. Uncertainty rules our lives today and as the lines between work and home are blurred by technology, we're reassessing our relationship with work and the organizations that provide it.

If the connection between workers and their work requires more from them than a pick-up, put-down eight-hour stint, then it needs to give them a damn good reason to be there. Increasingly, as balance erodes, work needs to integrate more seamlessly into our lives. Our experiences with the businesses and organizations we work with is a huge part of that. Workers, as end users, need a high-quality experience, or like their commercial counterparts, they will go elsewhere to get it.

I was recently speaking with the head of human resources for a UK manufacturing organization notorious locally for its less than favourable treatment of employees as anything more than paid labour. She reported the regular occurrence of workers not showing up for work and not calling in sick or otherwise. On contacting them, sometimes after a number of attempts, they'd nonchalantly say things like *I've left* and *I'm working somewhere else now.*

Of course, this lack of loyalty and adherence to proper procedure causes consternation within the management, although there is no change in the way they treat their people, or operate their organization. Their approach is not about enabling people to do their best work to achieve the aims of the business, it's an antiquated belief that their workers should be grateful for a wage and that they are there to do nothing more than the basic tasks they are told to do.

The old models of work and ways of organizing it were designed for suppression and control like this. These two mechanisms, applied today, prevent the adaptivity, responsiveness and ability to innovate quickly that are required to compete. The way it's always been is no longer an option.

Our organizations can no longer deliver business aims in the most effective way through linear rigidity. They must be dynamic, evolving systems – a reflection of the world they exist in. In short, they need to be alive!

For many years the customer has been king. Customer service, customer experience, customer retention have all been major areas of attention over the past few decades and it remains true that if no customers turned up tomorrow, there would be no business. We're starting to realize though that it's equally true that if no one turned up tomorrow to serve those customers, there would be no business.

Every business has one thing in common – people. You can remove or change any other aspect of an organization, be it environment, equipment or anything else and still be in business. Combining this with the increasingly consumer-like choice we have today as workers, it's clear that organizations are all about people. Without people, there is no organization!

Since the Industrial Revolution, organizations have been trying to use humans to undertake robotic jobs, turning individuals into numbers to repeat tasks again and again. Now we have robots to do the robot jobs. We need people to be people – it's what they're best at and it starts with allowing them to be just that. People are not assets, or resources – they are people and we need to start realizing and recognizing the benefits that treating them as such can have.

Do the right things – for the right reasons

If we all used this simple mantra to guide everything we did, the world would be a better place. It implies a level of consideration in behaviour and to some extent, a level of ethics. In this age of uncertainty, we're finally starting to recognize the negative impacts we're having on the world and the problems that decades of rampant capitalism have caused environmentally, socially, economically and politically.

Because all resources are finite, models based on infinite growth are destructive and crazy. Traditional linear models of organizations that base success purely on growth in finance and scale are equally ridiculous – yet still they prevail.

Just as common logic came to realize that the world was round in the first place, so it's coming to realize that a relentless drive for nothing above profit is hugely damaging. Cheap clothing from a store in London, on the face of it, seems like a great thing, but consider the working conditions and treatment of workers required to produce these goods at a price that still leaves room for profit, as well as the environmental impact of materials and processes used to manufacture and transport them. The real cost is much greater, but it just doesn't show on a balance sheet.

In 2013, the collapse of the eight-storey Rana Plaza Building in Dhaka, Bangladesh killed over 1,200 people. It was reported that after cracks appeared in the walls the day before and the building was closed, garment workers were ordered to return to work the next day (The Fifth Estate/CBC, 2013). Under pressure to supply fast fashion items to the West, these workers paid the ultimate price.

Practices like these aren't infinitely sustainable and while the mechanisms of development slowly improve such situations, that they are allowed to exist in the first place is tribute to a profit-first mentality that has pillaged the world of its natural resources and treated workers as less than people since the Industrial Revolution (and before). No business making the right decisions for the right reasons would let such negative impacts happen. Profit can come as a by-product of doing business with conscience, but when it's the number one driver, it comes at the cost of everything else – even human life.

Worse still, we let it happen. As consumers we have choice, as workers traditionally less so, but that is increasingly changing.

It leaves a conundrum though; if people chose not to buy these items, the negative impacts of their production would be reduced with falling demand, but then the workers (poor conditions and all) would be even less able to support their families, so poverty would increase further, making them more likely to take terrible jobs with poor conditions. It's a huge symbiotic mess that needs to be unravelled, but it's starting to move onto the agenda.

The recent rise in businesses with conscience, who base their approaches on doing the right things for the right reasons show that profitability can come with a genuine belief in doing the right thing. You can bet that every one of the fashion companies outsourcing their manufacturing to Rana Plaza have corporate social responsibility programmes and charity affiliations, but do they genuinely think about the ramifications of all their actions beyond whether they can achieve higher profits?

The people tied to and affected by an organization include, but go way beyond, those on its direct payroll. For example, consumer demand shapes the actions of smartphone makers' well-treated employees and has a knock-on impact on the communities that mine the precious and rare metals required to build the electronic devices they design (*The Washington Post*, 2016). Thankfully, positive impact is as powerful as negative.

In June 2016, the UK-based healthy food for workers startup Lunch'd took to the streets to actively seek out homeless people and provide them with a healthy meal. Using surplus ingredients that would otherwise have been discarded by business necessity, the gesture created positive impact, which in turn enhanced the reputation of the company with zero spending on PR.

Every day, tonnes of perfectly edible food is thrown out by major retailers. It makes you wonder what taking positive action on this could achieve for their business. Doing the right thing for the right reasons pays off – and not only via karma.

With the growth of accountability through technology, good and bad practices are starting to be highlighted first-hand, without the filter of organizational PR. Supermarket food waste is now well-documented in the UK and people are taking action to address the situation, applying pressure on the retailers. On a larger, global scale even fashion manufacturers and brands can be found behaving with genuine conscience.

They're actually benefiting from it too. Doing the right things, for the right reasons is morally and ethically rewarding and it creates advantages that can be measured in traditional business terms.

CASE STUDY

On Black Friday 2016, clothing company Patagonia donated 100 per cent of its sales to non-profit organizations working to protect the environment. That equated to $10 million, five times their expectation.

Consumers got behind the idea because they believed in its positive impact, and knowing Patagonia as a business that bases its ethos on activism and positive impact, the offer was recognized as authentic, not gimmicky. As a result, Patagonia achieved something amazing and contributed positively to the world around us, all while following their mission statement to:

Build the best product, do no unnecessary harm, use business to inspire and implement solutions to the environmental crisis.

From a traditional business perspective, Patagonia's Black Friday actions seem crazy. The idea of a brand giving away its entire sales on one of the most important shopping days of the year is just not in keeping with profit-first wisdom. It certainly wouldn't please traditional shareholders.

Look at it the other way, though. Patagonia wanted to do something in keeping with its founding beliefs and in acting to its principles attracted more customers and greater loyalty to its business. The resulting coverage, exposure and goodwill generated by this act could not have been generated by an additional $10 million added to the marketing budget, because what happened here was a genuine connection between a business and people. It's a case of Patagonia doing the right things for the right reasons – and benefitting from it.

By doing the right thing, your business gives people, both customers and workers, a reason to believe in it. People congregate where they believe.

As we'll see later in the book, applying a little thought and doing the right things for the right reasons can also create a positive impact in the workplace itself, drive amazing leadership and help shape your simple, better, human organization.

Making a connection

To encourage people to congregate around your business or organization, you need to give them something to believe in. There has to be a reason for people to buy from you or to work for you.

Price or salary can be a factor that attracts people to transact with you, but it doesn't foster loyalty and therefore will never create a lasting connection or a relationship that remains strong over time.

A strong connection between an organization and its people has many benefits. If a connection between an organization and its workers is based purely on salary, the offer of a better salary will tempt workers elsewhere. It's a temporary, transactional relationship where work is exchanged for money.

When the connection is based on a common belief or goal, there's a shared mission which leads to a deeper, two-way bond that offers more to all involved. People are more deeply invested when they believe in something – they care about making it succeed.

In a saturated world, where we're all faced with information overload, to succeed, our organizations need to stand out and create a connection with the *right* people – those who believe in its mission. It's the only way to cut through the noise and make a real connection. There are myriad opportunities for transactional relationships, but authentic connections based on shared beliefs are necessarily rarer and as a result, far more powerful.

Installing a slide in your workplace, or a ping pong table in a meeting room just because you've seen Google or another funky startup do it, doesn't make it right for your organization. Just as people thrive best when they're true to themselves, organizations do too. People look for something genuine to connect to; they need a reason to align.

Relationships based on connection rather than transaction are more productive, more forgiving, more sharing and more committed. Why would a worker voluntarily respond to e-mails or flex their hours to support a business beyond their basic contractual obligations without reason? If it meant doing something they really believed in or were passionate about, they would choose to.

There is no great separation between the way things work in our personal lives and the way they work in our professional lives. The dynamics of relationships are the same wherever people are involved, so the drivers of success are the same too. As a result, building an organization has more in common with the principles of operating a functional household than creating a formalized system which requires people to adapt to operate within it and sacrifice much of their personal individuality for transactional gain.

The human workplace is one based on real, human connections. Connections we recognize and connections that recognize us. A great challenge for any organization is understanding how to foster that connection to ensure it has three fundamental things:

- the right people;
- in the right places;
- doing the right things.

There is nothing more to any organization than these three things. All that is required of any organization is to get them right. Creating an opportunity for the right people, place and action are all it takes to succeed and that all starts with a connection. When you get this right, everything else falls into place, but to do that you need to develop your organization in a far more open, collaborative and participatory way, which requires a lot of letting go.

It's a question of stripping back the layer of complexity and getting back to the fundamentals of what you do, why you do it and how. In itself this isn't easy. Many managers have justified their positions and reinforced their positions by adding complexity, while often workers mark their contributions by adding extra tasks to procedures, paragraphs to policies and levels of committee approval. All of this complexity masks the real reason why the business does what it does and how it does it, reducing the opportunity for those genuine connections with the right people to occur.

Why make it any more complicated than it needs to be?

CASE STUDY

Making the connection: interview with Kirstin Furber

BBC Worldwide is the main commercial arm of the British Broadcasting Corporation (BBC). I spoke to Kirstin Furber, people director about what it takes to connect a complex, dispersed organization with people who share its beliefs, why it's important and to learn more about how she continues to develop the human aspects of this workplace.

My ethos around calling myself a people director is about enabling people to be themselves at work. Companies today need to understand how, in the challenging world with multiple pressures and external forces, that can be balanced with business aims.

My belief is, that to best enable this, the organization must:

- be clear of the direction;
- involve people in that;
- make sure they understand and can buy in personally;
- facilitate and manage their views and feedback.

Focusing in this way allows people to congregate around purpose. They gain a common understanding of what needs to be achieved and to actually achieve it, people need to be themselves. That's core to operating now and into the future.

Most companies now are starting to think about how to transform from rigid corporate hierarchy to allow the flexibility needed for people to be themselves. It's an exciting time we're in! There are tangible business benefits to making this shift, too. When people *want* to work, they're able to contribute far better and by unlocking different thinking and deeper contributions, the organization can unlock new potential.

BBC Worldwide is a creative media organization. It has always needed to innovate to stay competitive, but today and into the future every organization needs to innovate to adopt the same mindset. Choice is allowing people to become much more fussy as consumers and employees, so they need to be given reasons to buy from or work for a specific organization. If you're not happy, you're not going to be able to do your best work, or want to engage. When that happens, the organization misses out on ideas that could lead to potential opportunities. Everyone has ideas and thoughts, so they should be able to bring these to work.

It's harder for more complex, dispersed organizations, because not everyone is in the same place at the same time. Success is about balancing out giving people control and influence, creating or maintaining the connection with the organization, while aligning it with a bigger, over-arching perspective. It all has to be done at the same time and it takes time to do.

Clearly communicating, clearly engaging and defining purpose and strategy at the top strategic level is important. At the same time there needs to be the freedom for individuals and teams to apply these ideas locally and create the experience that allows them to do their best work towards that. Respecting how people do things is important and when you work globally, even though you might be using the same language, words might have very different meanings. You need to be aware of that.

Gone are the days where you have 'engagement in a box' that is distributed from a head office to the world. It's not authentic. Today we create a set of principles, then ask teams locally how they want to implement them for their own market and culture, making sure we have the mechanism to receive feedback.

At BBC Worldwide, when we were looking to build out what type of culture we wanted in the organization, we started by celebrating what was good, then identifying areas to build on. We went out to over 1,400 people across the organization, led by managers and leaders instead of HR and started conversations of all shapes and sizes that shaped our organization's commitment behaviours.

These behaviours were all agreed and refined as an organization, at all levels. Now, three years on, it's still really powerful to say that we did this together, rather than through a consultant or management imposing an approach. The values of any big organization will always be there and combined with an ethos and purpose, they can shape the organization. But with a clear vision of how we all behave, it's easier for everyone to understand and implement, rather than trying to interpret value.

BBC Worldwide behaviours and how they manifest

- *Clear direction*
  Leaders provide clear information on strategy and what we need to achieve, employees ask when they don't know.

- *Achieving business results*
  We know what our targets are and aim to achieve those.

- *Innovation and creativity*
  Openness to different ideas and risk taking.

- *Relationships*
  Giving honest and open feedback. Respecting different voices, opinions and diverse backgrounds.

- *Global excellence*
  Not one size fits all. Respecting different ways of doing things that contribute to this overall mission.

This is important, but rather than analysing it too much, you should be doing it. It's far more powerful when behaviours are used every day to provide practical feedback to everyone, rather than just staying as words on a PowerPoint slide. Organizations that aren't open to the human element and fail to recognize the wealth of knowledge and opinions their people can offer, risk missing out on a lot of potential positive influence.

Create a connection

Kirstin offers this advice for any organization looking to start on this transformational journey to connect with its people:

- be real;
- take a progressive approach;
- pilot first;

- engage people's opinions;
- take action;
- make it organic.

Treat people as you would treat each other. It's hard and it's not a question of being nice to everyone all of the time. Most important is being clear, transparent and honest about what's going on. People can make their choices and decide whether they're in or out based on this experience.

Thoughts on seriousness

I'm often amused by the unnecessary behaviours that pervade certain types of business, the unnecessary reinforcement of importance or status. Just by looking at the way workers act, or businesses communicate, you can get a feel for how they organize. Traditionally, the more formal you were, the more seriously people would take you.

Richard Branson was one of the first to question this with his informal approach and then-revolutionary refusal to wear a tie (as well as his penchant for a knitted sweater). The notion that formality means business has been eroding ever since.

As our organizations change to fit the world around them, the idea of the ivory tower is disappearing. In some of the world's most successful organizations, it would be difficult to distinguish the CEO from a trainee in terms of appearance and approach. That has many benefits when it comes to creating connections and encouraging open communication.

Now, more than ever, it's your actions, rather than your words that define whether people align with you. Authenticity counts above anything else in creating the right connection with the right people. I spent many years as a manager trying to adapt myself to what I thought a particular business expected of me. It was only when I gave in to my own informality and started acting authentically that I was able to form meaningful connections with my colleagues.

Seriousness and formality are fine, if they are authentic. They should never be forced and doing so serves no purpose other than to add layers of complication and misinformation. People connect with other people when they have something in common. Fake or token attempts to force connections are always found out in the end.

After all, why would you want to hang around with someone you had nothing in common with?

The organizations of the future are no longer machines or systems, they are movements. To make a successful human workplace, you need to start a movement.

What's the point, anyway?

Behind every great movement is a great reason.

Have you ever woken up to head to your futile job and wondered *why am I doing this*? Most workers have at some stage, and when people feel like this, their level of contribution drops through the floor.

The passionate people of Greenpeace, many of whom are unpaid volunteers, all believe fully in its cause:

> We defend the natural world and promote peace by investigating, exposing and confronting environmental abuse, and championing environmentally responsible solutions (www.greenpeace.org.uk/what-we-do).

They are activists, committed to this mission, passionately making their individual and collective contribution. It's unlikely that activists get out of bed wondering why they are doing it, because the mission is clear to them and it's why they align with their cause. The unlikely day an activist stops believing in the cause, is the day they stop aligning with the organization and go elsewhere.

The word 'purpose' fits well here and although it has become over-used to describe simple business mission statements rather than a genuine reason to inspire a deep connection with people, it's a recognizable idea so we'll use it. An organization's number one purpose is to ensure the survival of the business, then pursue its aims. Whether the business aims prioritize a cause or profit affects how the organization operates. It looks something like this:

$$\text{Purpose} = \text{Survival} + X$$

How an organization behaves, its longevity, impact and ability to adapt depends on how it defines its X.

An organization that pursues profit above all else, will find it harder to create a genuine connection with people and its relationships will remain transactional, regardless of the engagement, recruitment, retention, reward and recognition programmes it develops.

There's a spectrum where profit and cause are the two extremes. All organizations fall somewhere on that spectrum.

To understand where any organization falls on the spectrum, you need to consider what drives it and how it operates around that driving force. Use Figure 1.4 to think about where these organizations might lie:

- traditional financial institutions like HSBC and Barclays;
- Greenpeace;
- the UK's National Health Service.

Figure 1.4   Purpose is survival + X

SURVIVAL   +   X   Define Here _____

_____

_____

It's possible to make some profit while pursuing a cause, it's also possible to pay token attention to a cause, while focusing on profit. The question is true authenticity, because that real position on the spectrum defines who the organization connects with, how it operates and how it feels. Where an organization sits on the spectrum drives its behaviour, operation and ability to succeed in the modern world. It's interesting to consider that the extremes at both end of the spectrum are exactly that.

Businesses that organize around a profit-first purpose assume that perpetual growth is possible and focus on it. They act as if the world and its resources are infinite – and we know they're not. In these uncertain times, assuming constant economic growth and scale is dangerous and the wheels can come off very quickly.

On our tiny dot floating in space, everything is limited. Since there is only a finite number of people we can ever connect with our organization, it is prudent to concentrate on making that connection as powerful and strong as it can be while growing it to its natural maximum.

In an extremist organization, the power of a strong connection between organization and people is evident in the unrelenting pursuit of a specific aim. Extremism is destructive though and it's also slow to change and adapt, because of those unrelenting beliefs.

Positive activism, on the other hand, is exactly that. If your organization does the right things for the right reasons, it will attract the right people to it to form a strong connection and start a movement in pursuit of shared beliefs. It will make a positive impact ('positive' being defined in terms of pursuing a cause. It's worth remembering that what one movement defines as positive, another would view as the opposite!).

Where the right people congregate, they can achieve amazing things together, because they share a belief in what they're doing. Structuring an organization for positive activism is the optimum place to allow it to survive, thrive and (where it wants to) even make some profit.

The only way you get true activists is by giving people a cause to believe in and congregate around, without forcing them to believe that and that only. Providing the structure for this to happen is the purpose of the organization.

Purpose is a founding principle for any organization, it's why they do what they do. It's the basis of the connection with people – customers and workers and the fundamental principle on which the organization operates. It not only shapes the way the organization behaves, it provides the reason for action. It's the basis of their movement. Even if it's not consciously recognized, every organization occupies a place on the purpose spectrum.

They have to, because without purpose, there is no point.

Doing it

There is no specific way to create your own movement, adapt your organization or attract the right people. In fact, the great thing is that there are no set ways to make that happen. Finding their own way is what makes organizations individual, rather than carbon copies of each other.

Your organization has an infinite number of opportunities to be amazing. It has the potential to do that and is full of the people who can make it happen. What it may be lacking is two things: 1) knowing what amazing really is; and 2) allowing it to happen.

Moving away from traditions and being different, although traditionally seen as a risk, is the best thing your organization can do. Amazing is remarkable and nothing ever became remarkable by doing things the same way as everyone else.

One specific project I have worked on completely rethought a process. Implementing it would exponentially improve the quality of the service and in doing so would also save £250k per year against existing budgets. Having moved the idea through levels of committee, identified budget, selected a project team and getting everything set to start, final approval from the board was required.

As we went around the table, one by one, approval was granted, until we reached one person. 'I don't see evidence of other sites doing this and if we're going to do something like this, we need to know that at least five other sites have done it successfully' was the general gist of the argument, which was upheld. The project ground to a halt and the service continued to struggle, creating low morale for staff and a negative knock-on effect to customers. My alignment with the organization ended soon after.

Through being too scared to be remarkable and innovate, instead the organization held itself back. Trusting your people to do what you need them to do in pursuit of your purpose shouldn't be a risk. It should be a given!

While this book can show those at the top how to open up and give the organization permission to succeed, it also shows how positive activism at all levels can be very healthy. I can't outline every possibility, technique or approach your organization could employ to succeed, but I can highlight key themes and suggest starting points – real actions that you can take to create your human workplace.

The rest is up to you …

The evolve or die thing

The *evolve or die* mantra has become a staple of business bloggers over the past few years, but to some extent, it rings true. The world is no longer the same as it was and change is getting quicker. If your organization can't adapt to the demands of the world today and tomorrow, it will become obsolete. There are many famous examples of where this has happened already.

The demise of Kodak alongside the rise of Instagram is widely quoted as a classic example of evolve or die in progress, although it's misreported. Kodak didn't collapse completely. It went close to the wire, but its troubles were an example of how a behemoth that isn't set up to adapt as quickly as the world changes around it will struggle.

Today though, Kodak exists as a smaller, more agile and innovative organization, focused on products and services that fit today and tomorrow. As a result, it's returning to profit.

The previous version of Kodak was not in keeping with the world it operated in. Now imaging and tech are closely aligned, Kodak as a tech company has adopted the size and shape required for it to once again thrive and, as we've already seen, success isn't solely about size and scale.

There's a very famous quote from Henry Ford:

If you always do what you've always done, you'll always get what you've always got.

That's fine in a static world, but the world we live in today just isn't static! In today's world, doing what you've always done is no guarantee of results whatsoever. What created survival or profit for your business previously may create a loss today. Staying the same is the single most damaging thing a business can ever do, so it needs to organize itself to insure against that.

Being static is now far more dangerous than it was in a century ago when Ford made his statement. Right now, there will always be someone more agile, more innovative, more responsive and more in tune with its people than you. The playing field is no longer level and competition can come from anywhere – not just your traditional rivals.

To stay relevant, you need to compete in multiple ways:

- to have the best ideas;
- to bring them into the world;
- to iterate and reiterate as your audience requires.

All of this has to be done on a timescale that allows it to happen before the playing field moves again. Because the world is constantly changing, achieving relevance is not a linear project; it's a constant, evolutionary cycle.

Don't pull the rug

It would be very easy to read this premise, panic and tear your organization apart completely. You don't need to!

Admittedly, it's imperative to act fast, continuously and consistently, but that doesn't mean a complete rethink of your organization from the ground up. What it really means is unlocking your organization to behave in a way that's fitting for the dynamic, shifting world. It just has to allow itself to evolve and then continue to do so.

Doing that requires certain approaches and a change in mindset. It needs to become a human workplace – built around the people who work in, around and interact with it.

The most important factor in this is approaching it all with an open mind and interpreting the ideas that follow in a ways that suit your people and their purpose. The second most important factor is allowing it to happen. To do that, you need to recognize that this change isn't the responsibility of one person, it's owned by everyone.

Question: How do you define success?

Advice for other organizations looking to establish global communication, coherence and ownership

- Reinforce key messages constantly and consistently.
- Make sure everyone understands why you do what you do.
- Invest time and money in bringing people together.
- Involve people in the conversation.
- Walk the talk.

CASE STUDY

Building around ownership at CGI

To understand how a complex global organization, fuelled by consistent growth, can truly retain a deep connection with its people and form an effective global community, I spoke with Julie Godin, vice-chair of the board, chief planning and administration officer at CGI. Julie shared how a company built on a dream that puts people at its centre thrives in the modern world, offering advice for other organizations looking to do the same.

CGI has grown as a people-first company. Founded in 1976 by Serge Godin, who used his own savings to start a computer business, the company has grown rapidly and aims to double its size every five years. Today CGI is a global IT systems business, with annual revenues of over C$10 billion. From high-end consulting services, CGI developed through listening to its clients and understanding their needs. That close connection with people inside and outside the business remains a cornerstone of its ongoing success.

The philosophy of the organization was shaped by Serge's past and his experience, particularly early memories of his father losing everything when his uninsured sawmill burned down. He built CGI as a company for people, where they could come to build a lasting career and be an important part of its progress. Communication and collaboration has always been at the heart of the company.

Typically, organizations start with their vision, but for CGI, there has always been a dream to create an environment where everyone enjoys working together and can contribute to building a company they can all be proud of. By retaining this as the driver, the organization naturally keeps people as its central focus. Growing fast through mergers and acquisitions, CGI reinforces this *one culture, one company* idea to retain coherence across the global workforce. Integration is essential and the organization has invested a lot in building its Management Foundation Framework which provides the philosophy, dream, mission, values and programmes of CGI, to provide the guidelines for success. Surveying, questioning and understanding satisfaction of people internally and externally happens regularly, giving people ownership of CGI and its actions.

The Management Foundation Framework creates a core platform for operations and integration, that delivers consistency across the organization. Right from hiring, ownership is a big thing at CGI, which believes that as owners, people have the right to information and to be consulted. From joining CGI, everyone is made to feel that they have a say and that they have the platform to contribute and play an active part in creating success. This is the starting point for CGI.

The organization operates a decentralized model, which means all regions are managed by local leaders who are empowered to and accountable for managing their own businesses within the regions. The common denominator for all the business unit leaders in CGI is the Management Foundation Framework. It's a recipe book for how to do things, designed for consistency of experience for all leaders, regardless of where they are in the world, that reinforces CGI as one company.

How the CGI decentralized model works

- The regional location has to follow the CGI philosophy, set by head office in Montreal.
- To do that, local legislation and culture needs to be respected.
- The Management Foundation Framework layer is implemented as a set of principles, with that in mind.

Even within a decentralized model, technology plays an essential part in connecting CGI, particularly for collaboration and communication between countries and teams. The company invests in ensuring people can connect face to face, too. For example, the global operations meeting brings together all leaders of all business units around the world, every quarter. In this meeting everything from metrics, to best practice, to results are shared by the organization and the leaders themselves share their experiences, exploring how they can help each other in helping CGI progress.

The CGI 101 course provides a full week of training for all managers at all levels across the business, whether hired or promoted, in Montreal. It's an immersive experience, with presentations from all seven Presidents of Operations, as well as all corporate leaders engaging the participants in conversations. These are run three or four times per year and attended by around 300 people each time. It demonstrates how CGI values the connection between people and organization, at all levels. Once the work is done, the participants go back to their units to disseminate what they have learned, spreading the connection further.

Making sure that every level of the organization connects is an important part of CGI's identity. The principle of ownership remains consistent. All leaders take responsibility to provide the organization's governance information to their own teams and the organization ensures the platform exists to do that, while asking questions and making suggestions. Metrics are clear and made available to everyone at all levels, driving the coherent conversation, feedback, sharing and learning across the entire business. What great looks like is clear to everyone.

If leaders don't do it, why should they expect anyone else to?

Ten key ideas on the basics of a human workplace

1   There is no digital transformation, the world is digital by default.

2   Being able to respond to change before it's too late is essential.

3   Your business and organization are two different things.

4   The end users of your business are the customers.

5   The end users of your organization are the workers.

6   'Do the right things, for the right reasons' is a clear guiding principle.

7   A strong connection between people and organization is important.

8   Seriousness and formality are usually unnecessary.

9   Every business has a purpose.

10   Creating a human workplace doesn't necessarily require fundamental change in the structure of your organization.

There's no denying that the world today is different and the pace of change relentless. To be relevant and stay relevant requires businesses to think and act differently – they need to respond to the world around them. Doing that isn't a case of waiting until the world shifts, then doing something in response, the luxury of such a leisurely pace is over. The modern world needs human workplaces, built to be ready for whatever comes next!

Task 2: What's the point?

The business you work in, the unit within the organization, or your team each has an overriding reason for doing what it does. They are usually connected, but there are often subtle differences in this purpose at all levels. Use the ideas in this chapter to think about the purpose that congregates people in your workplace.

Business purpose:

Unit purpose:

Team purpose:

Personal purpose:

References

Frankel, T (2016) 'The Cobalt Pipeline', *The Washington Post*, 30 September. Available from: www.washingtonpost.com/graphics/business/batteries/congo-cobalt-mining-for-lithium-ion-battery/ [Accessed 17 April 2017].

Kelley, M (2013) 'Interview with jailed Rana Plaza Factory Owner Bazlus Samad Adnan', *The Fifth Estate*/CBC, 11 October. Available from www.cbc.ca/fifth/blog/interview-with-jailed-rana-plaza-factory-owner-bazlus-samad-adnan [Accessed 17 April 2017].

Savage, M (2017) 'UK vinyl sales reach 25-year high', bbc.co.uk, 3 January. Available from www.bbc.co.uk/news/entertainment-arts-38487837 [Accessed 17 April 2017].

Building your structure   02

The most fundamental challenge for any organization is how it should be structured to function as best it can in the modern world. There are certain things every organization needs to do:

- Survive today through delivering business aims.
- Survive tomorrow by continuing to do so, even if the prevailing conditions change.
- Believe in something that gives it a purpose above survival.
- Build a movement around that purpose.
- Turn the movement into an engaged, active community.
- Thrive through giving the community an opportunity to succeed by leveraging these things to ensure the right people, are in the right places, doing the right things.

This chapter explores:

- how organizations are communities;
- why free-flowing information is more important than worrying about structure;
- why we need to stop building companies and start building platforms;
- how when people thrive, organizations thrive too;
- how to get out of the way and let success happen.

Movements as communities

A movement happens when a group of people congregates around a shared set of beliefs. This can be transformed into a community when those people adopt common characteristics, practices and cooperation through their shared interest in the movement. Movement turns to community when it becomes organized. Every community has a unique social structure, based on the way it's organized around its purpose. From religious groups to social circles, book clubs to sports teams, anywhere where people organize around a common goal, a community forms.

What that community looks like is down to those involved. Sometimes the founding members decide, sometimes it's a wholly democratic process. The only thing that is pre-defined is that to succeed and thrive, the community must serve the needs of its members and enable them to pursue the community's purpose effectively.

Because of its unique purpose, each community is individual. The way it organizes around its goals is a reflection of its unique combination of purpose and people. So each organization should be developed on its own terms, with its own strategy and not only at the highest level via some predetermined universal model, but in its own individual way.

Because every organized community has a clear collective identity, each can exist anywhere, just by replicating the community's fundamentals of survival, purpose, action and organization. They can scale as globally, or remain as local as their purpose requires, while retaining their unique characteristics, as long as the community identity is strong.

The people that align with or congregate around your organization are its members. They are there to be served by the community, not to serve it. Their contribution is to support it in achieving its aims, rewarded by the ongoing experience of participation rather than a one-off transaction.

Every community has a structure and a focal point. These manifest in ways as unique as the aims, traditions and individual characteristics of the members, remaining coherent and allowing people to align with the community in a way that works. What this looks like in individual organizations varies widely – and rightly so.

When people thrive, organizations do too

If organizations are actually communities, the same mechanisms of success apply. Communities are built around people and the most successful ones are those where the collective power of those people is unlocked. When people thrive within communities, the community itself thrives.

But who are these people?

Traditionally, organizations have categorized the people in and around them in different ways – customers, employees, suppliers and so on. As a result, they treat these different groups in different ways.

Common business thinking says that the customer is the number one priority and that when you have a customer, you have a business. We've already seen that isn't the case, because if there's nobody to serve the customer, there is no business and after all, it takes people to create the customer offer before the business can even attempt to find a customer in the first place.

All of these groups of people contribute to making a business viable and an organization work. They *are* the community, with customers and workers being the joint most important, because without them there is instantly nothing.

More recently, there has been a recognition that by focusing not only on external people (customers), but also internal people (workers), an organization can thrive. The Virgin Group has famously viewed employees as its competitive advantage, recognizing that when their needs are being met, they do great things. Many others have followed suit, with the emergence of the employer brand idea in recent years signalling a recognition of the importance of selling the organization to employees. Originally ideas like employee engagement, recognition and reward were developed to help people thrive, but we're now seeing this move to a new level with the idea of employee experience – the real-life approaches that recognize workers as end users of the organization.

We've already seen how customers are the end users of the business and workers the end users of the organization (refer back to Figure 1.3), but it's not necessarily so clear cut. Where the community is organized effectively, the workers can (and should) also be customers and customers potential workers. The community's aim is to create loyal evangelists and spread the word as widely as possible. As a result, regardless of the point of entry, people can simultaneously be any kind of end user, because they are members of the community.

Every community member has a network of their own. It's always been the case, but through social media and other communication or collaboration tools, the size and reach of that network can be far greater and cultivated more simply than was the case even a decade ago. A great idea or cause can reach the right people in an instant, making a connection and drawing them increasingly closer to the centre of the community.

Take a look at Figure 2.1.

Figure 2.1 Organizations as nuclear communities

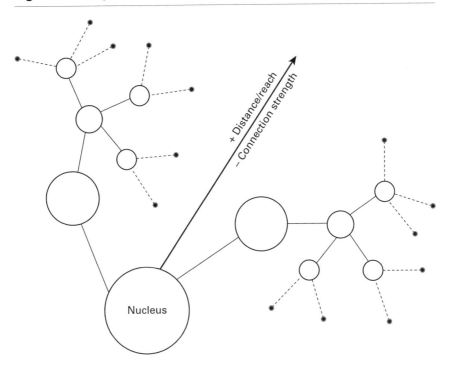

In the centre of the community is its nucleus. This is where the most passionate members congregate, where the bond is closest and loyalty largely unquestioning. These people are going nowhere as it's their life's work to follow the cause of the community. For this group, the organization is their life (or at least the unerring focus of their work).

One step out are the direct end users – customers and workers. Here the bond is tight and there is a common belief, but although these people may be passionate advocates, they are likely to have other, personal purposes to follow. People with families (communities or organizations in their own right) who prioritize the survival and thriving of that unit will fall into this category. They are committed and share the belief and aims of the organization, but they have other things going on too. For this group, the relationship with the community will flex more and may be less permanent.

The next step out is the wider network, or the reach of the community. It's where the message naturally spreads via the networks of both the community itself and the people that align with it. It's as far as those networks can spread. For someone with 1,000 LinkedIn connections, their potential reach is over 2 million and although many of those connections won't necessarily share the alignment with the community's aims, if a network is built to target only those who do align, it can spread its word far and wide.

The closer to the centre, or nucleus, of the community that people align, the more powerful their advocacy and their drive for its success. The organization's aim is to structure itself in a way that draws the right people (and as many of them as possible) to the nucleus of the organization, as the closer they get, the more powerful the connection. Let's take a look at Figure 2.2.

There's no surprise that this looks like a traditional marketing funnel. The mechanism here is to attract the right people to the community and bring those with the strongest connection as close to the centre of the community as possible. Customers, workers, whatever – it's the same mechanism!

Your organization doesn't have to appeal to the entire world, just the people who align with it, and it's more powerful when it targets only that group. The more successful it is at connecting with the right people and drawing them as close to the nucleus of the community as possible, the more capable and successful it will be.

The nucleus of an organization can be as large as is manageable, or feasible depending on parameters out of the community's control and how the organization is structured dictates what's possible. To be in the nucleus requires an enhanced level of connection – the ability to contribute.

The community is the source of input and opinion that is invaluable to the future of the organization. It provides the feedback against which it is able to develop and guide the business to adapt. It tells the business what its customers want next, or what its workers need to work more effectively.

Figure 2.2   Power of the community connection

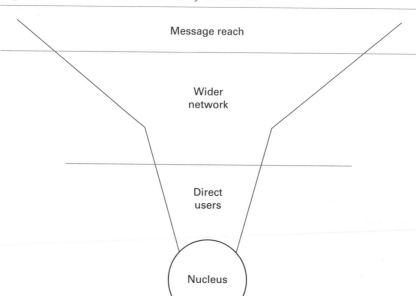

It's for this reason that employee experience has come onto the agenda for many organizations as an equal to customer experience and why its importance will only increase. It's also why organizations need to integrate their thinking even further and start focusing on a more holistic people experience. Customers, workers, suppliers, neighbours, they're all people and all part of the community.

When the community thrives, the organization thrives. The community is made up of people, so it's nothing only logical to say that when people thrive, organizations thrive too.

The problem with hierarchy (is not what you think)

If success for an organization (and as a result the business it supports) rests on how well its people thrive, traditional organizational development approaches pose a problem. This is illustrated in Figure 2.3.

Collectively, people are powerful. Because of the speed at which organizations need to innovate and adapt to keep their businesses relevant, future success rests in the power of collaboration. Every person within an organization's entire reach is a potential mine of insight, ideas and inspiration. Their experience of the organization, its products or services, its workers, customers and the world around it is individually unique. To succeed, all any organization needs to do is access that, by allowing everyone to contribute consistently.

People contribute when they are engaged or connected with what they are doing. The right people aligned with a community will naturally be inspired by its aims, so all the organization needs to do to get the best from those people is let them contribute under the mantra of doing the right things for the right reasons – acting in a way that contributes towards the aims of the business.

Figure 2.3 Imbalanced organizations with restricted information flows

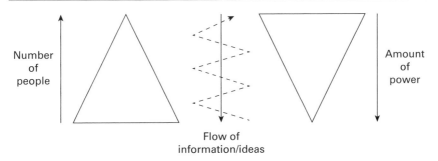

Number of people

Amount of power

Flow of information/ideas

That's why hierarchy, when rigidly reinforced, is a problem. The idea of a focal structure is in itself, not a bad thing. Even the most equitable communities have a figurehead and every community needs a nucleus to bond it together. The problem here arises when the structure of the organization is used to suffocate it, rather than keep it focused.

Traditionally, triangular hierarchy isolates, by placing the greatest power for decisions with the fewest people. Information is broadcast directly from the top, downwards, with no conversation.

If the knowledge and insight required to succeed rests with everyone, this isn't a great model. The majority of the insight and potential for ideas is repressed at the bottom. The flow of information upwards towards where the decision-making power rests is obstructed by levels of clearance. Although information flows directly down from the top, to get up there it has to perform a giant game of Chinese whispers.

> Gather a group of people in a room and invite a guest speaker to give them a talk on something interesting. While this is happening, set a game of Chinese whispers in motion using a genuine idea that could improve the business.
>
> At regular intervals, interrupt the speaker (it's helpful if they know this will happen, just for politeness!) and give out other unrelated facts relevant to the business.
>
> All of this reflects the operation of a traditional organization: a focus of attention, constant distraction and broadcast messages, the passage of time and the need for ideas to pass through level upon level of discussion and approval before reaching the decision maker.
>
> Once the Chinese whisper reaches the last person, see what the idea sounds like now. It will be nothing like the great – and possibly game-changing – idea you started with and it will have taken all that time and effort to lose its potential!
>
> I once tried this activity with a group of HR professionals at a conference. I forget now what the HR relevant idea we started with actually was, but by the time it reached the back of the room, it had morphed into something hugely offensive and mildly discriminatory!

The problem with hierarchy isn't the structure of the organization itself. In fact, simple hierarchy where the organization has a focal point is in keeping with the idea of a community makes a lot of sense. The problem is the way it's used to repress information and therefore hold back people's ability to

Figure 2.4   Unlocking information with dynamic circles

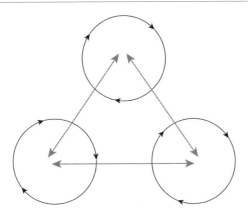

contribute in pursuit of the aims of the business. If an organization's key function is to allow people to thrive in pursuit of these aims, this is a huge failure!

To unlock creativity, innovation and success, all an organization needs to do is unlock the flow of information to allow everyone to contribute equally. It doesn't need to pull the rug from under itself and completely restructure, it just needs to allow information to flow directly between the right points in the organization instantly to support its own success. Doing that naturally turns triangles into dynamic circles (see Figure 2.4).

If the ideas needed to succeed come from the right people, in the right places, doing the right things, then stepping back and allowing that to happen through the provision of the right amount of structure and no more, is essential. We need to deconstruct the rules and restrictions that prevent full participation.

Our organizations don't need to be reinvented. All of the basic parts are present, it's just a case of unlocking the structure to allow people to be their best. As we move through this conversation into the actions that can make this all real, we'll discover how some of the most outwardly hierarchical organizations are unlocking the space to create, innovate and communicate. It's possible – you just need to do it!

Organizations as platforms

Every day, the majority of the internet-connected world interacts with platforms to enable many of the things we do. Loosely defined and borrowing from a technology perspective, a platform is a structure that enables actions to be executed (*Oxford Living Dictionaries*, 2017). Here are a couple of examples: 1) the operating system of your laptop – a place where code or software is executed; and 2) Facebook – the set of services, tools and products that enables users to create their desired experience.

I don't like the word *executed*. It's very clinical and abrupt. For the purposes of a human workplace, let's refer to getting things done as *actions*. The platform is where the action happens. It enables people to do the right things.

There are many misconceptions around platforms. You regularly see the memes doing the social media rounds on how:

- Facebook is the world's largest media company yet creates no content;
- Alibaba is the world's largest retailer yet holds no inventory;
- Uber is the world's largest taxi company yet owns no vehicles;
- Airbnb is the world's largest accommodation provider yet owns no real estate.

That's because all of these things are platforms. They enable their end users to undertake the actions they need to in pursuit of their aims, while helping to connect them and build their community. It's not a shock that they don't own inventory, because they are the enablers, not the executors, sorry, action takers.

This is exactly what we need our organizations to be!

Enabling action

Organizations need to enable businesses to survive and thrive, through enabling the right people, in the right places, to take the right actions. They need to act as community platforms, as enablers of action.

In designing an organization, the business needs to provide a set of services, tools and products that enables its community to grow and its people to support it in reaching its aims. It needs to be a utility to make people more efficient, relevant and successful.

The organization as a platform is the interface between the end user and the business. The experience that interface gives the users defines the connection between people and the business, allowing their shared purpose to happen.

This implies that organizations are services and are required to offer a level of choice, because people as individuals have their own preferences for interacting with the community, via the platform. They need to connect on their own terms and have an experience of that connection that works for them.

The people, place, action idea

If an organization is a platform, it needs to enable something. By stripping back what organizations actually need to provide to a business in order to help it meet its needs, at the most basic level, we find:

The right people

People who are aligned with the business purpose and able to contribute to it as a connected part of the organizational community.

The right place

Physical or virtual environments that enable the right people to do their best work in the most optimum way.

The right actions

The activities the right people need to take in order to contribute to the business mission and achieve the right outcomes to drive success.

Throughout the book we'll discover these ideas and work through making them real.

A personalized experience

As the world's largest social media (or media) platform, let's continue with the Facebook example. Both brands/advertisers and individuals are its end users. Some use it to play games, others to consume content, others for communication. It enables small conversations and interactions, as well as the formations of sub-communities and groups, all of whom form a part of the overall global Facebook community.

All users set their preferences as they go and are able to curate and build their own experiences within the services and tools offered by the platform. Facebook doesn't dictate how people should form their experiences, it merely provides them the tools to do so, within a minimal set of required parameters or guidelines. Anyone who stays within the guidelines can continue to use the platform in their own way.

This parallel with the function of an organization is even clearer when compared with a platform like Airbnb. It provides a simple-to-use interface that enables both those looking to rent out their property with those looking to rent a property via a set of tools to make that as smooth as possible.

Its users can curate their own experience to drive their actions – selecting how they list, communicate, search and more. The platform enables them to take the actions they want to take. Of course it has parameters, which define actions that are outside the scope of the community, ensuring that anything happening via the platform contributes and where it doesn't, that this end user is removed from the platform.

Rise of the platform organization

It's the same in organizations. Don't get Airbnb's external product confused with its internal organization, though. As an organization it applies the same platform thinking approach that it does in the product it provides – connecting and enabling through a quality end-user experience.

Increasingly, many of the world's fastest growing and best-performing organizations are adopting a platform approach – the natural way to enable a community to act in a way that pursues its aims. People are individuals after all and just as what works for one organization won't necessarily work for another, what helps one person to be their best, may hinder another.

The platform organization is more passive and less dictatorial than the traditional industrial organization. It provides a service to its end users, offering a choice that enables them to act in the most effective way to pursue their individual and collective goals within the business.

The right experience

For a platform to be successful, it has to offer the right experience to its users, supporting them to do what they need to do. The experience users have with the platform is absolutely essential, because that defines if, how and how well they use the platform.

How many times have you downloaded an app onto your phone, or started to use a new piece of software only to discover that it doesn't do what you need it to do? When that happens, frustration starts and we either stop using it unless we really have to, or delete it completely.

Just like any platform or enabler, an organization needs to help its users to better achieve their aims. In fact, it's the sole purpose of an organization. While the business has a purpose that defines what the community wants to achieve, the purpose of the organization is to provide the structure for that to happen.

Stop building organizations, start building platforms

Every organization is a platform that enables the right people to be in the right places, taking the right actions to achieve the business purpose. It's the interface between the people and the business. Just as in the world of software, getting that interface right to provide a quality user experience is essential to the success of the platform and in this case, the success of the business.

Organizations aren't just incidental, they need to be planned and designed to enable great work. To do that requires an understanding of the fundamental elements:

- Who are the right people?
- Where are the right places?
- What are the actions they need to take?

The basic principles of great organizational development are the same as the design of any great system:

- understand the need of the end users;
- be accessible and clear;
- be simple, recognizable and understandable;
- inspire trust.

Systems, or organizations, are designed for usability. They only exist to enable end users to do something, so providing the optimal experience for that is everything. The only way to really design an optimal experience is to design for people – start with the user's perspective. An off-the-shelf product that you attempt to shoehorn users into is a poor solution in a software purchase and a disaster in organizational development terms.

Designing for people as end users is the only way. If you want your people to succeed, create the experience that enables this.

Organizational user interface

Even if you follow these principles in every aspect of organizational development, there is still the point at which the people meet the organization, the ways in which they interact with it. This user interface is the gateway between the people and the organization. For them to fully play a part in the success of your business, the interface between the people and the enabling system needs to be high quality. A poor interface will lead to frustration, disengagement, staff churn and many other negative effects. It lights fires that then need to be fought!

The principles of the interface are the same as those of the experience. A touch point that inspires trust, creates a trusted experience. To really create a human workplace, we need to develop organizations as platforms that give people the optimal experiences to be their best, in their own way.

Beyond culture

There's a well-known quote from management guru Peter Drucker:

> Culture eats strategy for breakfast.

The problem is, it's wrong. Culture and strategy are part of the same thing. In fact culture *is* strategy – the manifestation of strategy in operation, anyway.

Culture is the social behaviour of a group of people. This means that organizational culture is the observable consequence of the connection between a business and its people. It's the result of great organization design. A good culture is the result of strategy – it doesn't happen by accident and in any case, 'good' as a general idea is ridiculously subjective.

If innovation and creativity are being blocked, it's because the organization is structured to allow that to happen. Anyone within an organization who blocks its ability to achieve its aims in the best possible way is an indicator that at least one of the organizational fundamentals is missing: 1) right people; 2) right place; and 3) right actions.

A blocked or ineffective culture is an indicator that the organization as a platform is malfunctioning – the system has a bug that needs to be designed out. It needs to be iterated as part of the constant non-linear evolution of the organization.

The definition of success and therefore good culture changes in line with the shifting expectations of the world – the context in which the organizational platform operates. Just as any platform is constantly iterated to provide the optimum user experience and therefore create the best possible results, the design of an organization is the same. If leadership has a genuine function in the modern workplace, it's to build and iterate the platform that allows the business to succeed.

You can't have a culture-first approach to building an organization, because culture in itself is an output, or consequence of actions. The purpose of a business defines what it aims to do; its culture is the manifestation of the way the organization builds the community around those aims.

What you can have is an organization built to function in a specific way and when it does that effectively, communal behaviour creates something observable – call it culture if you like. It's a measure of success of the organization, which succeeds when it's built people-first. When people thrive, organizations thrive too. Culture is the observable consequence of the connection between a business and its people – an indicator of how an organization is functioning and nothing more.

To create what many would define as an amazing culture, we need to create a people-first organization, a human workplace.

If it can't be tweeted, it's too complicated

Simplicity is always easier to understand than complexity. In structuring for simplicity, a quick win can be found in improving the clarity and simplicity of both communication and instruction. So, let's play a game.

One of the biggest bugbears in my working life is the length and complexity of documents like policies, procedures and contracts. I firmly believe that less is more and that, just like applying nothing more than the basic parameters to organizational structure, simplifying these documents down to core messages is far more powerful.

This situation is exacerbated due to these documents requiring annual revision. Often, the reviewer adds a paragraph here and there, to demonstrate to the approver that they have done something important. This adds an extra layer of complexity and year after year, the layers pile up.

They don't need to.

Commercial communication is simple, direct and all about strong messages that get the point across in the minimum number of words. All we need is for our internal thinking to adapt to match this. Policies and procedures aren't business documents, they're pieces of communication designed to inspire (or prevent) certain behaviours – just like marketing!

Find one of the most complex documents in your organization and see how far you can simplify it. See if you can get the key message down to the length of a tweet (140 characters). If you're particularly inspired, share it on Twitter using #Policy140. It's OK to share, collaborate with and provide feedback to others outside your organization, in fact it's natural human behaviour … but we'll come to that later.

Here are a few examples using common documents. If the organizational platform is set up correctly, they will work, because people will be connected and responsible:

- Health and safety: don't do anything dangerous or potentially harmful.

- Equality and diversity: treat every human as equal.

- Dress code: dress appropriately.

One of my favourite workplace quotes is the iconic Anthony Burrell letterpress poster:

> Work hard and be nice to people.

I genuinely believe you could build an entire organization on these principles! Try placing this phrase as the X in your business purpose equation and consider how it would change your organization if this was the fundamental driving behaviour.

Messages, like the organizations they support, need to be clear and simple. They need to serve a purpose, not make things more difficult.

Just enough structure to thrive

When organizations operate in triangles and require specific, restricted flows of information upwards through layer upon layer of approval, it's because they don't trust their people. This means one of two things: 1) they don't have the right people within the community in the first place; or 2) the organization isn't providing a platform that allows its people to thrive.

If you have the right people and give them the right platform, they will do the right thing. People doing the right thing don't need to be controlled, they can be trusted to get on with doing it, which in turn reduces the need for layers of management and approval (complexity), further releasing information and positive action to flow around the organization in the most suitable way, making it even more effective.

If the organization creates the right platform, everything works just fine. Relationships become easier, responsiveness becomes easier, the organization is naturally agile and innovative because it's plugged in – connected to the far reaches of its own community and the world beyond it. Most importantly, it's able to act far, far more quickly. Because conversation on this stuff tends to lean towards discussion of organizational models, it has become the preserve of certain thinkers, when in reality it's just common sense – treat people well and they will behave well!

Distrust requires level upon level of management. It's complex and it's hard, because when people aren't trusted, they get suspicious. Suspicion leads to disengagement both with the aims of the business and the task at hand. People are also individuals, so to manage them as a herd is always counter-productive.

A platform organization necessarily needs to serve people, by giving them the right conditions to thrive. Because a community is a collection of individuals, the more flexible and malleable it can be, the more it can create those appropriate conditions for every worker.

The more structure you apply to something, the more rigid it becomes. In a world where flexibility is key, rigidity is a disadvantage. When things change quickly, they're too slow to adapt and it hurts them. Look on it as turning the Titanic in the face of an iceberg that appeared from nowhere. No matter how badly people wanted it to turn, it just couldn't – it was too big, too rigid and too slow.

Human workplaces are not only more responsive, they are more resilient. Resilience does the same job as rigidity, in a far more effective way. It allows the organization to avoid the iceberg, or at least absorb the impact without breaking apart. When something rigid receives too strong an impact, it smashes.

That's not to say we should dissolve all organizational structure and create anarchy. There are certain benefits to structure of some kind. All good communities have a figurehead and a level of casting vote that rests in the nucleus and there are benefits to that. Whether a collective, a hierarchy, a holacracy, a wirearchy (ie an organizational structure based around networks) or just doing things in its own way, any organization needs to be designed to allow its people to thrive and to do that, there needs to be a level of guidance – just not so much that it suffocates the human contribution.

Know when to stand back

For a few years now, I've been speaking at conferences on the idea of 'just enough structure to thrive'. I know I didn't coin the phrase, although I have no idea where I osmosed it. I think Neil Usher, workplace director at Sky raised it in conversation, perhaps quoting social artist and founder of the Tuttle Club, Lloyd Davis. Wherever it came from, I'm grateful for it, because that short statement changed my entire view of organizations.

It cuts through the levels of complexity, the silos, the seriousness, the management, the jargon, the endless meetings – and so much more that is unnecessary in the working lives of so many people – with a simple message:

Do what you need to allow great work to happen, then stand back and let it happen.

My ex-wife is a portrait artist. When she paints, she develops a relationship with the canvas and the oils, working with them to evoke an intended emotion or response.

Knowing when to stop and move away from the portrait is a major skill. The temptation is to tweak and add extra detail, extra layers. Occasionally, this temptation is too great and a painting that was perfectly amazing can become overworked and lose some of what made it great.

While the idea that a simpler organization that trusts its people and enables them by creating just the right conditions for them to thrive is an amazing one, for many of us, raised on corporate culture and traditional business thinking, it's counter-intuitive. We're trained to be control freaks!

Simple and easy are not the same thing

Just because human workplaces are simpler, better and more human, it doesn't mean that creating and maintaining the platform to deliver one is easy. An amazing organization is a reward for effort and knowing when to let go is one of the most difficult aspects of creating one.

Once we do let go though, there are many benefits.

Human is natural

When people believe in the aims of the business and are given the platform to thrive in doing it, motivating them to do it is a natural thing. Complexity of structure is the biggest thing holding any organization back. By repressing people, the organization represses information, collaboration, and in turn creativity and innovation.

Complex systems are slower, take more energy and effort just to operate and are prescriptive in the way they work, putting barriers to better (simpler) alternatives. If you have the right people in the right places, doing the right things, there is absolutely no reason to control their every move.

I first became interested in the way organizations work after spending some time in the public sector, which is where I first encountered baffling, unnecessary complexity. Mainly, it was time spent in meetings, going round and round in circles with unnecessary conversation because people were not allowed to take action. This was an organization-level behaviour, defined by the platform and it's no surprise that today that platform is creaking almost beyond repair.

You can't force a human workplace. Any attempt to do so prevents the platform from being an inclusive, well-aligned community and instead it becomes enforced – a dictatorship. Forcible alignment with a cause is a completely different thing to a genuine connection.

These things aren't the preserve of the business world – evidence of them in action pervades anywhere you look. Governments, states, public services, education systems, institutions of all forms all highlight the differences between enforced participation and well-aligned connection around a common purpose.

When people are properly aligned and the platform supports it, they will pursue the mutual aims through the right actions. So an organization's role is, just as with the artist, knowing when to step back. Do just enough, then get out of the way.

Complexity delays innovation

Structure creates bureaucracy, which in itself means layers of complexity. This in turn means it takes longer for information and ideas to flow through the organization to reach a decision maker for approval (look back at Figure 2.3). It reduces speed, agility, flexibility and suffocates innovation.

Innovation, whether in products and services, or the way your organizational platform operates is the most important goal for all of us today. It's the only way to stay relevant in uncertainty, learn from failures and turn ideas into successes. Human organizations are naturally innovation communities, naturally reflecting the conditions for innovation.

A 2015 study by Schaffer Consulting unsurprisingly discovered that the four conditions leaders need to create to allow innovation in any organization are: 1) energy; 2) creative friction; 3) experimentation; and 4) just enough structure.

When an organization provides just enough structure and stands back, those other conditions are natural consequences of the opportunity it provides. Because when the platform aligns the right people, in the right places and enables them to, they *will* take the right actions.

When your organization is an innovation community, it will always be evolving, always innovating. When people take the right actions relentlessly, the right things happen to pursue the business aim.

Freedom within parameters

Understanding what the right amount of structure should be and when to step back can be daunting. Traditionally, businesses have organized around control. One of the principles of the industrial era was that work, broken down into small, repeatable tasks, could be done by anyone. As a result, organizations wanted numbers, not people. Gaps needed to be filled and as long as someone could potentially do the job, they were in.

This has continued over the years. The lack of alignment between people and business aims continues to mean that layers of control and approval (management) are implemented to force certain behaviours from people. The common approach to developing the organizational platform remains to start with control and then add elements of freedom.

Flexitime is a great example. Contracting someone to do certain hours, within certain times, then offering a level of restricted flexibility that often has no bearing on the individual's job, has very little positive impact on their working life.

What if there was a different way to look at it?

If, instead of starting with control and adding some token freedom, we start from the complete opposite point of view, we turn everything on its head and make it human, because suddenly our organizations become designed for people.

Complete freedom as a starting point

Let's start with complete freedom. A starting point where absolutely anything is possible – anything can be done in any way and it's up to each individual and team to choose what that is and how it's done. Already, we've created a whole new universe of potential.

Even if you aim to provide complete freedom, there will always be some absolutely essential controls that need to be taken into account. The things required to undertake the business's purpose safely, legally and (if required) profitably. Let's call these the parameters in which the business operates, or a task has to be completed. Through an approach of *freedom within parameters*, an organization can deliver just enough structure to thrive, while benefitting from the increased productivity, evangelism, creativity, innovation, efficiency and other benefits that come from operating a truly human workplace.

By removing rules and replacing them with parameters, the shift from control to trust happens naturally. Rules are prescriptive and restrictive, parameters are the basic conditions in which you operate. Parameters unlock and unleash an organization's people, rules suppress and repress them.

Freedom within parameters creates a focus on activity and gives ownership to people, allowing them to take responsibility for the things they do. It sees outcomes as a natural by-product of actions, can be applied to any aspect of organizational development at any scale and it works like this:

- Understand what the desired outcome is.

- Start with 100 per cent freedom, a blank page where anything is possible.

- List the absolute minimum of parameters that apply.
- Allow your people to define the actions required to create the outcome, within the parameters.
- Everything else is freedom.

This is illustrated in Figure 2.5.

To understand how this works in practice, let's work through a couple of examples, starting with a classic conundrum – unlimited annual leave. This is a sometimes contentious issue. Some organizations, like Netflix, LinkedIn and Virgin report a range of associated morale and productivity benefits. Others, such as Triggertap report a negative impact of trying to implement such a policy.

The desired outcome is that anyone can take all the time off they want to, whenever they want to, while the business continues to meet its aims. Starting with complete freedom means exactly that. Without any regulation, there is no guarantee that anyone will turn up and work on a given day. This definitely poses a potential risk to the functioning of the community!

This is where parameters come in. By asking what the basic conditions are that make business operation feasible, while leaving as much freedom available as possible to workers for taking leave, the absolute minimum of structure and absolute maximum of freedom can be applied.

Any organization might interpret this differently. When I applied this approach in my own business in 2013, our approach was that everyone could take as much annual leave as they wanted, within these parameters:

- The organization knows in advance.
- Your work is up together.
- You agree for someone to cover the very basics of your role while you're away.

With this absolute minimum of structure applied, unlimited annual leave worked for us, because with the parameters reinforced, it all took care of itself.

Figure 2.5 Freedom within parameters

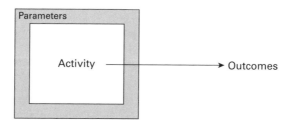

There is a level of contribution expected from any person participating in the community, which forms part of their alignment with the organization. If taking too much time off affects this contribution, their work won't be up together, so taking annual leave will not fall within the basic parameters.

The idea of freedom within parameters can be applied to any aspect of organizational life, as a way of understanding what the minimum viable structure is. In the case of flexible working, it supports the pursuit of activity-based, anytime, anywhere working, providing the essential parameters are applied. In a manufacturing operation, for example, one of the parameters may be the amount of time certain machines are required to run in a day. Another that they are tied to a specific location. Such parameters are what defines the minimum structure that allows the organization to thrive.

When I first came up with this idea and tried to implement it in my own business, I discovered a large caveat. It only works as part of an effective organizational platform, which in itself requires the right people, in the right places. On failing to implement activity-based working and understanding why, it became clear that the business didn't have a community – it had initially recruited people to undertake roles.

The connection between organization and people was missing and as a result, my attempts that first time failed. Connection is essential, because as much as all of this hinges on clarity and simplicity, it expects the organization and its people to trust each other. Without the right connection, it's hard to foster that trust!

Freedom within parameters works. Really, it's nothing more than basic common sense. Put the minimum structures and parameters in place, then allow people the freedom to undertake the right actions to achieve an agreed outcome. Because people work in different ways, that freedom supports each individual in doing what's right.

Where it fails, it's an issue with the organizational platform – a bug that needs to be removed from the system to allow it to function properly.

CASE STUDY

Insight: Nicola Hemmings, organizational psychology

As lead psychologist at Soma Analytics, Nicky is conducting the largest ever randomized controlled group study on stress in the workplace. With wider experience in supporting organizational development and growth through organizational science, Nicky's insight covers every aspect of the organization and workplace development spectrum. We discussed the connection between humans and potential human workplaces.

You can build trust with people around you and they can know what you're doing, but when you take advantage of that trust there can still be a feeling of breaking the norm – on both sides. Making sure you're doing good work is far more important than just sitting there to show presence and make an impression. It's essential to stay mindful of that. We're in a transition period where appearance is still important to many workplaces, while others are realizing that actual contribution is where true impact can be created. There are still a lot of people who enjoy the appearance – wearing the suit, the culture of 'being at work' – as much as making a connected contribution. From a worker perspective, as long as it's a choice, both ways are perfectly valid. It's up to individual personalities. Organizations are affected by the personalities of the people who founded them, with some exceptions, but these are the people who make the decisions. Whoever makes the decisions, shapes the culture. Organizations change as they grow too. The way they communicate, organize and deal with things has to adapt with growth and a lot fail to do this.

Organizations constantly shift and it's all about awareness:

- awareness of yourself and how you work at your best;
- awareness of the environment you're in;
- awareness of others.

We could be a lot better at awareness as humans. That's where we tend to act as machines. For example, when a colleague behaves in a certain way, rather than just reacting to the impact that behaviour has on you, being aware enough to understand what is driving that behaviour is valuable and human. *You've done X, so I'm going to do Y* isn't constructive or helpful for anyone.

Process has much to do with this. The more you add company processes, the more you take away autonomy, driving these X–Y responses. Processes as guidelines for decision are essential, but when they become dictatorial and proscriptive, we lose the human element and with that, gain destructive behaviours.

Many companies need parameters rather than rules, but they forget that and instead focus on increasing complexity through process. The idea of company values is becoming outdated, but the idea that you have a structure to make decisions within is essential. Things move so quickly, that strategy needs to adapt continuously. Providing a framework and set of guidelines that helps people to make decisions is extremely helpful. Giving the organization's identity, mission and behavioural guidelines provides a baseline expectation, allowing people the freedom to act in the interests of the organization.

Particularly in more complex, larger organizations, driving values and behaviour across the organization from grassroots as a community initiative is just too difficult. These things should start in the boardroom, because leaders have the overview and direction – they know the direction they want the organization to move in (and/or its individual departments), so they need to define what behaviours are needed to move it that way. It then needs to be properly implemented across the organization to let people know what they're doing and take ownership of those behaviours. That's the biggest part of innovation, letting people be autonomous. Letting people know where they're going and then giving them the autonomy to get there is powerful.

Recognizing how and why people align with the organization is important too. If people become too intrinsically linked to their workplace as a major part of their identity, they can be in danger of burnout. It also creates a huge echo chamber. Interaction with the outside world is of value to the organization, so allowing people to pursue their own purpose, while helping the organization achieve its mission it not only permissible, but healthy. From that starting point of recognition, you can start to create the environment where both people and organization can thrive.

We all make our own definition of what it is to be human. People and organizations are constantly working that out.

Your minimum viable organization

How successfully we tweak our organizations to remove the bugs that may arise defines how successful they are. The best strategies for doing this are through collecting and auctioning open user feedback. It's exactly the same way you would expect a software company to develop a platform.

What minimum viable means

The idea of *minimum viable* has been around for some time. First made popular by Eric Ries in *The Lean Startup* (Ries, 2011), initially it referred to product development, but it has come to be applied as an idea for creating businesses, launching startups and as a result, it works really well as an approach to building organizations.

This is my observed interpretation of how the idea can be interpreted for the Minimum Viable Organization (MVO). There are probably other versions out there that apply the idea to organizations and I make no pretence to own the notion, but as an approach to building an organizational platform, it works. *Just enough structure* and *freedom within parameters* are natural outcomes and it fits within a community perfectly. Here's how MVO applies to the human workplace.

An MVO is an organizational platform with just enough structure to allow its people to thrive. In operation, through the open information flow enabled by the reduced structure, it's able to gather constant feedback and insight from the people who use it, which highlights bugs, user interface and user experience improvements that, when addressed, allows the organization to continually evolve and improve to meet the needs of its people.

Because an MVO is an organization constantly in development, it is set up to evolve and change. The simplest way to enable this is by making the organization's structure as simple as it can be – why waste time, effort and money developing, implementing and sustaining additional elements that just aren't needed to enable the business to thrive? After all, if a business survives and achieves its aims, that's all it needs to do. Anything else is complexity and complexity blocks the direct path to success!

Understanding what your people need in order to thrive so your business can do the same is a necessary part of being an MVO. This means continually designing, prototyping, piloting, testing and tweaking the solutions, even when the solutions are fully rolled out. It's an organization that iterates. An iPhone 7 is recognizably an iPhone, yet through feedback-based iteration, it is far more advanced than an iPhone 1, not because it has a huge raft of complicated additional features, but because it adds and removes features each iteration, based on what will improve the interface and experience for its users.

Adoption of ideas

In product terms, the adoption curve (Rogers, 1962) is how minimum viable is rolled out through its community. A similar curved model of adoption exists for ideas and developments within an MVO. Take a look at Figure 2.6. The connection between the organization and its users is strongest at the evangelist/champion end where opinion is not only positive, but potentially comes with positive activism to support its spread. The fence sitters and passive blockers are key to shifting the weight of popular opinion in favour of the idea and once the tipping point is reached, any noise from active blockers is muted. Evangelists and champions are the groups most likely to provide active feedback as well as spread the feature through the community.

Figure 2.6   How ideas spread

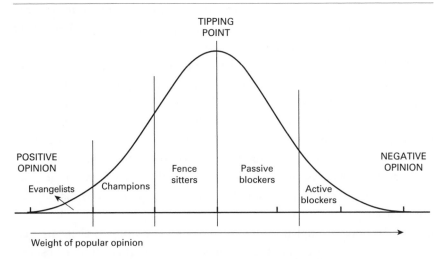

SOURCE Adapted from Rogers, E (1962) *Diffusion of Innovations*, Free Press

For an MVO, achieving adoption of an idea is a circular process. Ideas are tested (piloted) in a specific part of the community, where the connection is strongest, revising via feedback, before gradually being rolled out through the community to its furthest reaches, iterating as more feedback is received from more users.

Delivering the right platform features

Let's call the things an organization does *platform features*. All an MVO needs is the basic features required to achieve its purpose and no more. By testing the features where the connection is strongest, the platform can be tested in operation and improvements made without alienating those on the periphery of the community. By piloting in this way, the organization can then avoid the huge potential costs of a failed implementation, because it avoids creating features its people don't want or don't need.

Fluid iteration

It's a fluid process, too. Iteration continues during roll out until the feature fits the community, or until feedback determines that it's just not required. Features can come from anywhere too, because successful implementation is all about adoption. Even if you're the most junior, or newest member of a team, you can launch an idea – your mission is to have it adopted by ensuring it benefits the community.

The more the flow of information is unlocked within the organization, the faster and more seamless this process can be and the more adaptive and quicker moving the organization will be too.

Minimum viable is the natural way to deliver just enough structure to thrive. It's a great mantra for anything in life – do the minimum required to succeed. Anything more is unnecessary!

Design thinking

Minimum viable organizations are designed, not developed. Design is a never-ending process that drives and is driven by every aspect of the human workplace we've seen so far. With the simpler, better, more human approach of designing organizations as communities enabled by platforms, comes a new mindset. As ridiculous as it sounds, that mindset is little more than common sense.

Right at the very start, we touched on the changing nature of product and service design, as well as the rapid changes in consumer behaviour that are part of the shifting requirements placed on businesses. Structure-light, adaptive approaches based on minimum viable everything are cyclical, rather than linear. They iterate, rather than replace. For organizations, this means they are designed as opposed to developed. When something is developed, it implies that there's a point where it's fully complete. The process of modern design is ongoing.

Unfinished organizations

Our organizations are never finished. The moment an organization stops constantly evolving, it becomes linear and out of sync with the world around it. We need to constantly design and iterate the platform to enable the people in the community to thrive.

I'm often asked to run design-thinking workshops for teams to help them innovate, collaborate and create more effectively. Design thinking is widely used in product and service design today and it can equally apply to organizations. If organizations are platforms with end users, in designing them we're effectively designing products. It's no huge leap to realize that what works in product design, works in organization design.

There are various interpretations of design thinking theory, my own follows the simplest way it can be implemented to be effective. In fact, it's simple common sense.

Organizational design thinking

For organizations, design thinking is a set of five steps:

1 *Understand.* What are you trying to create? This could be a problem that needs solving, a process within the organization, the organization itself, or anything else that requires action or attention. This insight comes from a connection with your end users. The community will tell you what it needs, as long as you allow it to.

2 *Think.* Before taking action, take some time to understand the community insight and what it may mean. Really understand what might be needed in order to meet the need as you have come to understand it. This is where ideation techniques and alternative perspectives are really useful.

3 *Design.* Take your ideas and turn them into a potential solution to the problem that can be practically delivered in the real world.

4 *Make.* Create a prototype – your first iteration of the solution, the minimum viable.

5 *Test.* Launch it within your community, as close to the nucleus as possible for starters.

This is an open process. By ensuring the community (at an appropriate level) is able to contribute feedback and discussion at every stage, the data available from real users is live and available for constant tweaking. Use this feedback to iterate.

At any stage of the process, you can go back to any other stage. If users provide feedback at the test stage that requires a rethink of the solution, go back to design. If that feedback actually shows you don't understand the need, go back to that stage.

Design thinking is constant, collaborative, community thinking. It's fluid and the more open your business allows it to be, the more powerful it can become, since the more people who contribute the greater the input of ideas and perspectives.

As the basis of constant innovation, it seems like obvious logic that design thinking should be the default setting in every aspect of our working lives. After all:

- Why would you launch a feature that no one wants?

- Why would you roll out a solution universally before piloting it?

- Why would you ever assume something is 100 per cent finished?

Yet somehow, every single day, organizations from the smallest to largest operate in a restricted way that suffocates innovation. Organizations that fail to plug into their people in this way miss countless opportunities to improve and progress.

Just like our products and services, our organizations are never truly developed. They are a work in progress and to know what improvement looks like, we need to gather insight and feedback from the very people who will be using them.

Perpetual beta

Remaining unfinished is not a bad thing.

When we were working in lines, with a determined start and finish point, getting to the end was important. It was proof of arrival. But we know today that the world is cyclical. The end of one cycle is the start of another and every cycle is part of a larger one.

Evolution is constant and change in the world outside our organizations is relentless. To succeed they must constantly adapt. If we ever assume that we're at an end point, we're standing still. When we stand still, we fail to keep pace with what's moving around us and lose ground in the battle to stay relevant.

Community, platforms, just enough structure, minimum viable, design thinking – all of these things fit, enable and require constant mobility to succeed. Most importantly, to succeed our organizations need to have the right people, in the right places, doing the right things to pursue the purpose of the business, at all times.

When people thrive, organizations thrive too. To build a human workplace, we need to rethink our organizations with people at the centre. In an uncertain world, that requires constant adaptation. When we believe we've arrived is when we lose our relevance.

In product development, they refer to the process of gathering open feedback by allowing a community to use the product in the real world as beta testing. This is what our organizations need to do perpetually. It's the fundamental part of creating a human workplace.

Ten key ideas on structure

1 Businesses are communities, built around people.

2 Organizations are platforms.

3 User experience (UX) connects people to the business; the user interface (UI) provides that.

4   Culture *is* strategy (and we don't need to worry too much about it).

5   Simplicity is essential if people are to understand what they need to do.

6   Provide just enough structure for people to thrive.

7   Freedom within parameters is a universal framework to unleash action.

8   A Minimum Viable Organization (MVO) is all that is required, nothing more.

9   Design thinking is the mindset that enables all of this.

10   Every organization is in perpetual beta.

We can now take these fundamentals of organization design and develop a platform that unleashes people!

Task 3: unleashing freedom within parameters

Complete the freedom within parameters diagram below for any area of your organization where you would like to focus on increasing performance by unleashing people. Consider:

- *Freedom.* Your starting point is that there are absolutely no restrictions.

- *Parameters.* What are the absolute immovable factors that need to be considered?

- *Outcomes.* What is the required by-product of unleashing people in this way?

- *Actions.* What needs to be done to create the by-product?

Figure 2.7   Freedom within parameters worksheet

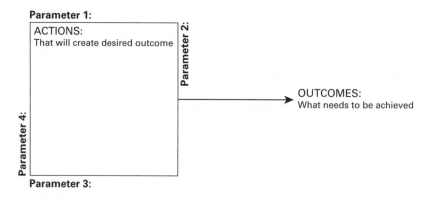

Remember, the more parameters you add, the more complexity you add too. Complexity stifles opportunities for thinking and acting differently, prevents fast moving responsiveness and also makes things more boring for everyone!

References

Ashkenas, R (2015) 'Four conditions that leaders create for innovation to thrive', Forbes.com, 22 April. Available from: www.forbes.com/sites/ronashkenas/2015/04/22/four-conditions-that-leaders-create-for-innovation-to-thrive/#9ebf8dc4b599 [Accessed 17 April 2017].

Dictionary definition of 'platform' from Oxford English Dictionaries. Available from: https://en.oxforddictionaries.com/definition/platform [Accessed 17 April 2017].

Ries, E (2011) *The Lean Startup: How constant innovation creates radically successful businesses*, Portfolio Penguin.

Rogers, E (1962) *Diffusion of Innovations,* Free Press. Adoption curve version here adapted from an original idea in this text.

All about people 03

If you understand the genuine value of building your organization people-first, then you understand how people are the most fundamental building block of any successful business. Just as we need to attract the right clients, we need to attract the right people.

Conventional business wisdom will tell you that finding and working with the *right* customers is essential, as these relationships are more loyal, more productive, easier to manage, reciprocal and generally happier. It's logical that if you're working with an individual, team or organization who you genuinely connect with and share common understanding or beliefs with, the work you do together will be better and creating success will be far simpler. That's because it's based on a quality relationship.

This chapter explores:

- why people are the single most important thing for any business;
- finding, keeping and unleashing the right people;
- how personal purpose comes before company purpose;
- why behaviours are more important than values;
- the importance of real diversity.

The main thing

We all know from our personal lives both the positive impact that strong relationships have and the negative, destructive impacts of bad ones. It's a simple fact – bad relationships make our lives worse. We need to take that realization to work.

Just as it's a brave step for an organization to refuse potential business by structuring so that it only works with customers where the right connection exists, so it may be that the leap of faith is even more pronounced when it comes to bringing people into the organization's community as workers.

Holes and wholes

When we're overrun with work, when things need doing and when there's a risk of not delivering a level of service, quantity or quality of product we've promised, the pressure to get someone in to fill a vacancy is huge. In these cases, one of two things can happen: 1) we fill the vacancy with the best person we can find as soon as we can find them; or 2) we wait and leave it empty until we find exactly the right person for our community – someone we really connect with.

In the short term, just getting someone in seems prudent. We can fill a gap in the organization and start working, keeping output levels closer to where the organization needs them to be. That may be so, but if we've hired someone for their ability to undertake a specific task, rather than our shared connected belief in the organization's mission, there's no guarantee that connection will ever be there.

Someone who isn't connected fully with the organization will never be a fully integrated into the community. As a result, they will never be fully connected with the work they're doing in it which means their contribution will not be what it can be. Worse still, a disconnected worker can be a destructive influence within a community, as well as bringing bad habits into their work.

The fact that 87 per cent of the global workforce is disengaged (disconnected) from their work and/or their employer (Gallup, 2016) shows just how badly wrong most employers are getting this simple requirement. At home, we avoid bad relationships and suffer when we don't, so why at work do we think that they will ever work?

People are the fundamental building block of every business's ability to achieve success. The right people, in the right places, taking the right actions, enabled by communication and technology are the only things any organization exists to create and it all starts with people.

People first

If you don't have the right people in the first place, everything else is irrelevant – your organization will never be the best it can be, regardless of size and scale. In fact, the startup traits that seem to be the holy grail for larger organizations today (look back to the Introduction for details) are exactly those that reflect having the right people – the energy, commitment and shared drive to achieve the business aims that come when passionate people form the nucleus of an emerging community.

There seems to be a magic number around 50 when startups start to struggle in retaining that early energy, because structure needs to be added to account for the growing size of their community. We paid attention to it at BDG architecture + design, while friends at startups from Yammer to Mind Candy reported the same. Usually, this is the risk point, where that community identity can be lost as scale is given priority over connection, yet this is the most critical time where the wrong move can derail the entire business, due to the magnification of effects that come when the wrong people are brought into a community they don't connect with.

How they get there in the first place is a cause of some consternation. During a few years in recruitment, I struggled to understand the mechanisms in play. Organizations targeted potential workers based on their knowledge and experience of a specific task or role above anything else, rather than how they aligned with the business. They then enticed those people through a financial offer. It was work as a transaction. Where the balance of power lay in these negotiations depended on the supply of labour versus the demand for those skills. It was never anything more than a trade of skills and time for money.

That's not to say it didn't work, but often the quality, longevity and productivity of these relationships weren't what they could have been if the organization had connected with the right person in the first place. It's not that our organizations are entirely unable to function with the wrong people in their midst, it's just more difficult for them to be their best.

Quality of relationship

When the connection between people and organization is less than optimal, additional structure is needed to make sure people are doing what is required by the organization. As with any bad relationship, there is no trust and with the lack of trust, comes complexity. Management and structure are the organizational equivalents of checking a friend or partner's e-mails and phone messages to see what they've been up to, or choosing their clothes for them so they wear what we want them to.

Personal relationships like this never last (and quite often end messily!), so why would we make this our default workplace relationship setting? The single most important thing any organization can do, is create relationships with the right people – it's the only way to build a strong community nucleus.

To paraphrase the famous saying from Dan Jacobs, head of talent at Apple, 'I'd rather have a hole in my organization' than the wrong person. Chris Baréz-Brown passed that nugget to me in our conversation, which you can read later, and Jacobs' quote is easy to find on the internet.

Despite sounding flippant, it's a very insightful perspective on building organizations around the right people. It's better to be single than in an abusive or dysfunctional relationship. Pure common sense tells us that when we align with the wrong people, the wrong things happen. It's time we stopped doing it.

When the entire way many of our organizations find and keep people remains based on the industrial age ethos of *anyone is better than a hole*, we have a problem. The organizations addressing this problem in the most effective ways are those achieving greatest success, because they understand that a community connected around a common goal can achieve great things together. These things aren't achieved by blanket and broadcast, it's a two-way street.

Building a community around a business requires the creation of an organizational platform that offers the right UI and UX to create that connection. As ever, *connection* is the key word. Human workplaces are all about people, because without people, they know they don't exist.

CASE STUDY

Schneider electric – an interview with Diana Bacanu, global wellbeing leader, and Paula Aitkenhead, global wellbeing specialist

Schneider Electric is proud of its award-winning Global Wellbeing Programme. As a large, multinational, complex organization operating across many cultures and locations, bringing change at company level is a challenge. Implementing a wellbeing programme and Cool Sites workplace initiative was unique, adopting a bottom-up approach that involved Schneider's people. Diana and Paula explained the programmes, why wellbeing is important to the organization and the positive impact the focus is having on all aspects of the business.

The Wellbeing Programme
Wellbeing is at the heart of Schneider's mission to become a more human-centric organization. With 144,000 employees across the globe, we needed to start by benchmarking to understand what wellbeing means from one individual or country to another. We use the insight to identify a Schneider definition of wellbeing:

'*To be healthy, be happy and make the most of your energy at work and at home.*'

It's a whole view of people as human beings. Wellbeing is linked to energy and people's ability to perform, so it's a holistic view – physical, mental, emotional and social. If you learn how to make the most of your energy in these dimensions, you will bring your best self to work and be able to contribute your best work. It's a move from engagement, where people are willing to give their best, to sustainable engagement, where they are both willing and able to. There's an understanding that this is also part of the organization's social responsibility. Happier, healthier people at work, will also be happier, healthier people at home and in the community.

At Schneider Electric, we had to create a framework for cultural change, while leaving individual countries to be empowered to take their own actions around them. This framework was formed around five pillars:

1 Health and wellness: inspiring and enabling healthy behaviours and lifestyles.

2 Flexibility: adapting to people's needs for a better work–life integration.

3 Physical workplace design: creating energizing spaces that enable wellbeing.

4 Leadership: great, caring, and inspirational leaders = chief energy officers.

5 Global culture: how the company fosters wellbeing as part of its DNA.

What makes this approach unique is that it's more than a project. It's a strategic initiative part of our company programme aiming for 2020, so it's on everyone's radar as a focus. Schneider's view is that wellbeing drives engagement and engagement drives performance. There is a clear, direct link between wellbeing and traditional business performance.

From the beginning, it has been a collective journey. We started with a blank canvas and co-designed the programme with our employees.

The programme design process:

- *Think tank.* Creating the five pillars in workshops.
- *Global crowdsourcing campaign.* 100 days where everyone could contribute ideas.
- *Building a community of champions.* Volunteers who ambassador the programme.
- *Project teams.* Programme design around the pillars.
- *Executive role-modelling.* Demonstrating commitment.

There is huge diversity in people involved in the project. It's a shared responsibility. The organization, its leaders and its people are all empowered to own wellbeing and contribute. It's a major key to success. Twenty per cent of what is being done is this high-level strategy. Eighty per cent is local implementation. This is also part of the journey of empowerment.

Internal and external data is showing that the programme is having a huge effect. The employee engagement increased significantly in the past two years (+6 per cent) thanks to the wellbeing programme and is now higher than market average by 5 per cent. External recognition is also coming, with the programme receiving a number of awards around the world. In addition, the ongoing development of the movement is being driven by Schneider's *Wellbeing Labs* initiative. This empowers teams to create wellbeing actions around what is most important to them, whether physical, mental, emotional or social. The philosophy is that if everyone takes little actions consistently, it will drive the big change and in just six months; 550 labs were voluntarily created across the organization.

By creating the space where people are permitted and encouraged to have ideas and innovate, the energy generated creates real impact. Around the world, people are experimenting and piloting ideas around wellbeing. From working standing up, to planting communal gardens, there is a constant stream of possibility that can be shared with the wider organization and give others ideas for their own location.

Cool sites

A programme designed from scratch in 2012, the idea was to create a workplace where people would want to be. Not workplace design at this stage, but the softer, human focus of bringing everyone together with information and coherent ideas. Schneider's sites host different business units and this was a way to avoid the silos that were starting to emerge, while promoting the re-emergence of a community spirit.

The aim was to empower site directors to bring people together around events, services, healthy habits and initiatives. The ambition was to make it people-focused rather than site-specific. Again, this programme was driven bottom-up, by understanding what sites offered for their people. The people decided whether their site met the *cool site* definition and were empowered to implement as teams to improve their own daily lives on sites.

By the end of 2016, 115,000 employees in 385 sites in 60 countries had adopted and developed the programme in a way relevant and adaptable to them. Each year, sites have to re-qualify and data has shown that those who reach second or third year consecutive cool qualification have up to 8 per cent higher engagement levels, which has a known correlation with higher performance.

Cool sites has now adopted the physical, mental, social and emotional wellbeing drivers to explore how the site where people work at encourages them to take care of those aspects of their own wellbeing. It has now become the backbone of our workplace design policy which allows us to take the programme a step further by incorporating human aspects into the physical design of our workplaces, which impacts hugely on performance.

Sharing the stories generated by these programmes is essential to Schneider, enabling others around the world to share the experience, gain new ideas and perspectives for their own workplaces and contribute feedback to work being done. Due to the 80 per cent local implementation approach, the variety of ideas are valuable and contributing to business outcomes. This isn't a glossy PR initiative, it's a purposeful, impactful programme for the entire organization.

Purpose

We've already looked at the purpose of the organization and the importance of people connecting with it, but how does that fit with their personal life purpose, which is likely to be a priority? Schneider Electric have recognized this in their initiatives and organizational development consultant Kevin McDougall spoke on the subject at All About People 2016 (see the references section for a link to his excellent talk).

For Kevin, as a husband and father, the overriding purpose is creating a great life for his family. Part of that purpose is working to provide for them. In order to contribute fully and to the best of his ability, Kevin needs to work in a place where he connects with the aims or the organization, the work he does within it and the impact that creates for himself and others. Although his personal purpose is not identical to the purpose of the BBC, Kevin aligns with it and therefore contributes actively as part of the community.

Different people need different things. We all have our own quests, goals, values and meaning in our lives. Everyone wants and needs different things, but can come together and congregate around the things they believe in.

By accepting this individual purpose as part of who a worker is, an organization can receive additional benefits from their contribution. A cult member is as repressed as a worker in a controlling organization. An aligned community member, however, retains objectivity.

Where that objectivity is given opportunity to contribute, through the open flow of information up, down and around the organization, the alternative perspectives that – multiplied by the number of individuals – enables is a powerful force. It brings the power of the community into the organization and truly forges the connection, allowing the business to access information and ideas it needs to stay relevant.

With ideas being the commodity they are in the modern workplace, the more individuals, with the more perspectives that contribute towards a shared goal, the greater the potential they bring. If this notion of individuality alongside shared goals becomes ingrained in the way the organization finds, keeps and unleashes its people, it truly becomes a human workplace and the business itself becomes truly unique – an individual – because no other business receives input from the same combination of perspectives. Allowing for individual purpose first, while aligning around a shared one, is a powerful thing.

Recognizing purpose in this way means that diversity in all forms is embedded by default a positive influencer. It prevents the recruitment of carbon copy people, which so often happens in organizations that eulogize about culture. The more diverse a workforce, the more potential that organization has to deliver the organizations purpose. The narrower the criteria placed around what a member of the community should look like, the lower the potential combined contribution. It goes back to freedom within parameters – the more you apply control to any aspect of an organization, the less human it becomes and the less able it is to succeed.

Going back to reducing policies to tweet length, as we discussed in Chapter 2, how about an equality and diversity approach which amounts to 'Recruit individuals who align with our goals'? That leaves nearly 100 characters for hashtags! Things don't need to be any more complicated than they need to be.

In my experience, organizations that focus single-mindedly on culture above all else and attempt to absorb their people wholly into the organization, so that it defines their lives (not integrates with them), become one-trick ponies and create as many problems as they solve. I'm not comfortable singling out smaller organizations, but the Zappos example, by expecting a cult-like worship of and immersion in the organization, proves the point. (I'm comfortable calling them out as the company has already been sold to Amazon.)

Where culture building around an unequivocally shared purpose exists and that purpose is the success of the business, the fervency is unsustainable. These organizations then move on to preaching their leadership approaches as gospel truth in the notion that the way their organization operates is the way all organizations should.

The individuality advantage

That's not the case. Organizations are individual, because the people within them are individuals. Collectively, they can share a purpose, but it is not the only factor at play and a human workplace understands that. Allowing people to be who they really are and embracing the positive impacts that can bring is essential.

Just as the right people need to integrate with the organization to form a community, the organization needs to integrate with the right people to really form a productive connection.

The right person could be anyone who aligns and, by keeping barriers minimal, the possible participation of anyone from any group, orientation or background you care to mention becomes open. When every aspect of an organization is approached freedom-first, it is naturally people-first.

CASE STUDY

Perspective: the benefits of true diversity

In conversation with Toby Mildon, diversity and inclusion lead, Deloitte, formerly at the BBC, we discussed the connection between people, organizations and the benefits of individuality in true diversity. These are his thoughts.

Workplaces don't exist without humans. Even if we lived in a world – and perhaps we're going that way in the not-too-distant future – where workplaces were made up of robots, humans still have to be involved somewhere in the process. To humanize work, we need to understand we're talking about people, not machines. It's a move away from the industrial way of thinking, but we're in a world where humans should be at the centre of workplace design.

Carbon copy people

Unconscious bias is an industry within itself today. One of the fundamentals of my work is that, in recruitment, we've realized that humans are hard-wired with unconscious bias. It's almost human nature to recruit in our own image. Unless you're particularly aware of this and proactively building a process to avoid it, you are at risk of hiring in your own image.

This is very common across many organizations and creates a lack of diversity. We know that, while diversity isn't easy, diverse organizations outperform those that are homogeneous. Studies have shown this to be the case financially, creatively, in problem solving, reaching new markets and customers. That's what's at stake.

Cognitive diversity

When I talk to managers about diversity, it's very easy to think about diversity in terms of affiliation to groups. The colour of someone's skin, their gender, physical abilities, sexual orientation. Today the conversation is moving on to cognitive diversity and when it moves to this approach, the diversity problem becomes much easier, because people can relate to that. We are all diverse, so not only are there the major diversity groups, it's like an onion, there are many more layers – educational background, where and how you were brought up, thinking styles, introversion or extroversion. There are many different combinations, but cognitive diversity sticks and we need that in the workplace to be creative.

If you're not careful, you risk alienating the straight white middle-aged man and that's not the aim – diversity needs to include everyone. By focusing on cognitive diversity, the issue becomes more accessible to everyone. We are all cognitively diverse and that's an idea people can easily get their head around.

Starting points
It's important to understand that diversity is a given. The world is diverse and so many businesses are global, so diversity exists. The question is whether the organization chooses to include or exclude. Acknowledging diversity exists and respecting people's differences is a starting point, behaving in an inclusive way.

Beyond recruiting, quite unwittingly, many business processes can be exclusive, so looking at everything from an inclusivity perspective is essential.

Large vs small organizations
Larger organizations have a keen appetite on diversity and inclusion because of the way it reflects on their employer brand and they often have the money and resources to invest in it. In smaller organizations it's potentially easier to be agile, but unless the leaders are serious about inclusion, they won't do much about it. A small tech startup hiring a small team of developers is more likely to just call their mates and select from a closed pool of people like themselves. It needs commitment to ensure that by recruiting through networks we're not reverting to less diverse recruitment practices.

Avoiding box ticking
Tokenism is easy and needs to be avoided. Often you find in organizations that managers feel diverse because, for example, they might have someone from an ethnic minority background within the department. But when you speak to that person, you discover they went to the same university and have exactly the same background as everyone else in the department. The genuine cognitive diversity is missing. On paper, the organization feels it's meeting requirements, but in real terms it's missing the opportunity presented by genuine diversity.

Responsibility for diversity
It's both a leadership and wider responsibility. We know that in larger, more complex organizations, this diversity doesn't just happen by itself. You really do need it to be championed from the top. At the same time, change can happen from the ground up and from within, but the leadership needs to own the agenda too.

Diversity as standard
Diversity doesn't naturally happen. Take the UK for example. We exist in a diverse place, yet organizations don't often reflect the diversity of the areas around them. Rather than viewing an individual as part of a diversity group, we

need to start leveraging the diversity of the individual and organizations aren't there yet. We need to help them get there.

Organizations can build approaches, tools and processes to enable themselves to mirror the communities they operate in. That helps ingrain diversity into the organization as standard, although it's deliberate, as opposed to naturally occurring. Until we can make it natural, we'll continue to see the workplace inequality we've seen and the organizations will suffer.

Why are most FTSE100 companies run by white men at board level? Diversity is on the agenda, but it's neither standard nor natural yet.

Where to start

For an organization that is just starting on its diversity journey, Toby recommends the following priorities.

Understand your starting point

Know the diversity of your workforce so you can understand where to put your time, money and effort most effectively.

Get genuine buy-in from your most senior people

If the most senior leaders don't get it, pay lip service to it, or treat it as a box-ticking exercise, it will fail. It needs the leaders to genuinely believe in the value of diversity.

Understand where bias occurs in your organization

Look systemically at where bias exists across the organization. For example, are there aspects of your recruitment programme that favour specific groups, or are certain types of people more likely to be promoted? Start by fixing these first.

Behaviour not values

If *connection* is a major word in defining a human workplace, alongside an updated view on purpose and culture, we also need to rethink the idea of shared values. The values of a person are the standards they live by, their vision of what they see as important, the drivers of their behaviours. These are our fundamental individual beliefs and that makes them something specific, something that shouldn't necessarily be aligned to an organization. In fact, the idea of shared values is a strange one in the first place.

For an organization to declare values is one thing, but the way this idea has manifested across the corporate world seems to be a board-level of declaration of 'corporate values'. In this respect, the idea of shared values is nothing more than tokenistic. Stencilling specific words onto brightly coloured walls, adding a list to the About Us page of a website doesn't actually mean anything.

Values are the drivers of behaviour, not the behaviours themselves. Just like the idea of a 100 per cent shared purpose between business and person, the idea of 100 per cent shared values is misleading and pointless. Do we really expect the fundamental beliefs of every member of our community to be identical to those of the organization?

Even if we do and could recruit unerringly to this list of shared values, doing so would restrict the incoming flow of individuals into our community to nothing more than a set of carbon copies. By reducing alternative perspectives, the opportunity for creativity and innovation reduces. What you're left with is a group of people who agree on everything.

Values are one of two things – meaningless tokens declared from the top, or straitjackets that remove the potential for individuality. To build a truly human organizational platform, what we really need are real humans, individuals, given the parameters of a set of behaviours the community expects them to commit to.

Committing to a set of behaviours allows for the retention of individuality, as they don't need to be connected to our fundamental beliefs if we're able to display them. If we're not, we're not the right fit for the community.

Buffer, the social media scheduling company operates a completely remote workforce, spread across the world. Rather than employ a set of prescribed values, it recruits individuals who subscribe to a set of 10 behaviours that all Buffer workers are expected to display.

The Buffer behaviours

1 Choose positivity.

2 Default to transparency.

3 Focus on self-improvement.

4 Be a no-ego doer.

5   Listen first, then listen more.

6   Communicate with clarity.

7   Make time to reflect.

8   Live smarter, not harder.

9   Show gratitude.

10   Do the right thing.

By applying this parameter of behaviour, the minimum of structure is applied, leaving the organization free to hire individuals who align with Buffer and its mission. It's a clearer, more measurable expectation that can really mean something. Asking people to manifest values is ambiguous, almost impossible to measure and too leading to offer real value. Dave Chapman did an excellent job of telling the Buffer story at All About People (see the References section for a link).

Whether your organization decides on values or behaviours, remember, these are parameters – part of the structure of your organization. The point of that structure is to give people a platform to thrive and it needs to be as minimal as possible. Adding confusion adds complexity, which removes potential.

Think carefully about what behaviours you want your community to subscribe to and don't dictate them – give everyone ownership of the process. We'll cover change later in the book, but any major definition or decision is far more effective, impactful and seamlessly implemented when the people it affects are part of it. Dictating from on high implies a level of detachment that undermines the strength of the connection between people and the organization.

Contribution over attendance

We already know that technology is enabling us all to work in new ways. Each of us has the potential to be connected and productive 24/7, but that doesn't mean we should be.

In the UK during 2015–16, the Health and Safety Executive reports that (Labour Force Survey, 2016):

- there were 488,000 cases of work-related stress, anxiety and depression;
- 11.7 million working days were lost to these conditions.
- main factors were cited as workload pressures, deadlines, too much responsibility and not enough support.

While technology is untethering our work from a specific time and place, we haven't yet either adapted our behaviours as workers and managers, or updated our organizational platforms to account for this.

In the main, employment contracts are still based on a number of hours of work required per week. Even when this is disconnected from specific times or places through flexible working, these documents still specify 'normal' working hours and a minimum number of hours.

This is at complete odds with the way we naturally work and as a result, the work–life balance of many workers is spiralling out of control, to the detriment of themselves and the organizations they work for. Sleep deprivation alone costs the UK economy £40 billion, US economy $411 billion and Japanese economy $138 billion per year (BBC, 2016).

Just because I'm physically or virtually present over a specific timescale, it doesn't mean I'm working. Equally, just because you can't see me, it doesn't mean I'm not. Presenteeism, where although physically at work, a worker may not actually be contributing, is an increasing issue, with the CIPD Absence Management Report 2015 suggesting its annual cost to business is twice that of absenteeism (CIPD, 2015).

The effect of traditional hourly based employment is to penalize those who work in a way that enables them to be their most effective. Where we're contracted by hours of presence, someone in the workplace during working hours and not working, is of more value than the person working outside the office at differing times when they're most able to deliver the activity they need to.

Measurement by contribution and activity over attendance is a better match for the working world of today. Moving to it needs the adoption of freedom within parameters.

There's no doubt that some jobs need to take place in a certain place at a certain time. On-duty schedules, transport timetables and manufacturing machine operation requirements are a few examples, but in each of these there are opportunities to unleash work in some way within the basic, immovable parameters – it just takes a bit of rethinking, within the context of that specific organization.

Business success is achieved by the right people, in the right places, doing the right things. It's not achieved by non-specific people, showing up somewhere specific during specified hours.

Finding people

Having removed the barriers to bringing the right people into our organization, we need to find them. Traditionally, this was a reactive process, but the changing world means a changing approach. We're not just finding people anymore, we're finding the *right* people.

As it was, a vacancy wasn't person-shaped, it was skill shaped. If an accountant left, the aim was to replace them with an accountant. The same way the case for any job title you can think of. The tasks required for a role were listed, an advertisement placed and a process began to identify someone who could do that specific set of tasks.

The problem is that this is one-dimensional and a very short-term solution. A person may be able to do the job, but when they're recruited on that basis, the wider connection with the community is of secondary (if any) concern. When the connection is ignored bad things happen, because loose connections disconnect easily. Worse still, when they're hanging on by a thread, they can cause all kinds of problems. Just think of the house fires caused by badly connected electrical wires!

The loose connection issue

We can define a loose connection as someone who:

- is not fully aligned with the business purpose;
- is not fully connected with or enabled by the organizational platform;
- does not, or is unable to participate to their potential;
- is not actively open to improving the situation.

Loose connections are more likely to either leave the organization, or cause disruption and a lack of productivity. Both outcomes are expensive in financial, time and morale terms.

In my experience as a recruiter, companies looked to fill a task-shaped hole above all else and anything positive the postholder brought with them was a bonus. It's why job descriptions continue to be formed as lists of key responsibilities, with a person specification bolted on to the end featuring words like 'tenacious'.

In order of importance, the selection criteria for a job tends to be structured in this way:

- skills;
- experience;
- knowledge/education;
- personality;
- aptitude.

In a human workplace, the benefit comes from contribution via a genuine connection, not solely whether you've done that job before somewhere else. This is important for a number of reasons. Hijacking a leading salesperson from your direct competitor is a dangerous game. You're recruiting their skills and experience, which could include both bad habits and an alignment with your competitor rather than your own community. If bad habits and loose connections are brought into a community, the strength of the community is undermined.

It's easy to argue that this is more pronounced the higher the skill requirement for a role (because how much contribution can someone working a production line *really* make?), but that's not the case. Working as quality control in a food production factory, I received an overview of the dynamics of that organization. Disconnection between people and organization, as well as levels of seniority, caused problems with morale.

In areas where morale was high, less wastage occurred, fewer staff issues were reported and the harmony in the workplace translated into care for work and commitment by all involved. Seemingly little things like cleaning and preparing for the next shift to take over rather than running for home the second your shift finishes, make a real impact on output and, down the line, profitability.

Regardless of the skill level, the more connected a person is with the organization, the more they contribute to the community. That connection comes from alignment through beliefs and behaviours, which are things an organization can't change in someone. Your employer can't change who you are, how you behave, or your aptitude.

An employer can give its workers knowledge, skills and experience. In fact, they start providing that from the moment a person starts working with them – or beforehand if they're clever. From the first interaction with the community, the organization has the opportunity to offer related knowledge to people and it can give them all the skills and experience they need once they start work. It can't change who someone is!

This begs the question – why do so many organizations still try to recruit people through an upside-down method? The right people create the strength in any community. They align, contribute and form the basis of success. So, every organization should be focused on finding the right people, above and beyond all else. That starts with who they are and how capable they are – the two things the organization can't give them. When those things are in place – the basis of the connection – everything else is secondary. Previous experience can be a bonus (but also a hindrance), but it should never be there driving force of recruitment.

People-first recruitment is the basis of a human workplace. Find the right people, bring them in, give them everything they need to contribute and thrive.

Job descriptions

If traditional job descriptions are upside down and ineffective, do we really need them? Rather than proscribing tasks and responsibilities, it's better to offer the right people an outline of their role in the community using freedom within parameters.

You can't expect to effectively find the right person using the combination of a traditional recruitment advert and a document that focuses on task over personality. You need to find the *right* person and the basis of that connection is in your organization's individual identity. The only answer to recruiting is creating an individual approach.

To attract the right person (or people), you need to create the right connection. Just as a brand or product creates a connection with a consumer through a shared set of beliefs (whether price, quality, vision, or anything else), communicated in the right way to not only reach, but engage the right person as a customer, your organization needs to create the same connection with its potential workers.

Look at the formal job descriptions you use – do they really appeal, excite and connect, or are they mundane lists of facts? Look at how marketing messages are put across – they use the appropriate platforms, media forms and messages to appear to their targets. That's what your recruitment messaging needs to do.

Approaching it this way moves recruitment from an administrative, process-driven task, into a creative project. It also never stops.

What's in a title?

If you're recruiting people before skill sets, does it really matter what their job title is? Traditionally, a level of social and organizational status has been gained through job titles, but we live in a world of contribution.

If we need our people to contribute rather than just show up, not only do we need to de-formalize the structures they operate in (even if we keep the structures in place), we need to remove barriers to the flow of information. If job titles imply unreachable seniority, they act as an obstacle to the emergence of the idea that could shape the future.

Over recent years, we've seen much evolution in the idea of a job title. First things went crazy one way, with unnecessary formality. From refuse collection operatives to beverage dissemination officers – guess what these are! – unnecessary complexity disguised the fact that these were people, doing real things.

As the internet age bloomed and the idea of disrupting the old ways gained traction, things went the other way. Digital overlords, light benders and marketing rockstars emerged to save us all. Equally confusing, but really, none of these things matter. It's who you are, how you contribute and how you connect that dictates impact now. Try changing your job title on every e-mail you send for a week and see if it makes any difference at all.

Titles are good for showing trends. More subtle changes like the shift from human resources to people management and now employee experience are great ways of documenting this transition from transactional business–worker relationships to the new community age. This is external though – for doing your work and achieving success, it really doesn't matter what you're called, as long as you're the right person, in the right place, doing the right things.

Don't focus on unnecessary detail, focus on what really makes a difference in building your community. If that's a job title, think about it, if not, it really doesn't matter. In a relentless world, getting things done the right way is what matters. How you define that doesn't.

Talented communities

Why wait until you have a vacancy – an empty slot that is causing operational problems by remaining empty – to engage the right people? Just because recruitment has traditionally been retrospective, it doesn't mean that is the most effective way, particularly in today's world.

We already know your organization is a community and part of its purpose is building that community. Connecting with the right people is a fundamental part of your organization. Marketing does that proactively, making sure the right people are ready to consume the right messages, engaging with the brand and ready to become a customer when the time is right.

The attraction funnel

This is exactly the way recruitment needs to function in the human workplace. Communicate – bring people into your community, in the same way marketing does. Customer or worker, both are people and those connected with your brand and aligned with its vision are already part of the community. They are the right people.

It's then a case of finding the opportunity for the right people to be in the right places, doing the right things. Finding a suitable position for them and bringing them towards the nucleus of the community when the time comes.

Building a connected community has a number of benefits. It's an early screener and selection tool, it puts people before skills or experience and when the time does come to bring a new person in, they are ready and waiting to go.

Creating that connection and building the funnel is the fun part! It's nothing more than Figure 2.2 in action and it's up to you to develop an approach that works for your organization.

No one is better placed to match an individual to an organization than the community itself. Moving your recruiting approach from reactive to proactive is not only more enjoyable, it saves time and money in recruiting costs, staff turnover, lost productivity and more.

Develop your approach!

CASE STUDY   NBC Universal Talent Labs

Daniel Zumbrunnen is director of talent development at NBCUniversal. He leads the global design, development and delivery of all high-potential experiences at the NBCUniversal Talent Lab, from early career through to executive level talent. Here he shares more about the Talent Lab and the importance of high-potential talent development programmes.

What is Talent Lab?

The Talent Lab is our suite of learning and development experiences that are uniquely designed for NBCUniversal. They develop leadership capability, enhance media business acumen, and help shape and define our culture.

Our work meets NBCUniversal talent where they are in their career, with experiences that align them to the company and their role, build needed skills within the media industry, or accelerate our talent to invent the future of media.

We don't serve 'employees' or 'team members', rather we view those that join us as 'talent'. And we don't preach in classrooms or at a university. We connect our talent in interactive, immersive and experiential labs that encourage testing, failure, practice and innovation.

How does this fit within an organization as complex as yours?

The Talent Lab actually helps break down some of the complexity of the organization. Part of our purpose is to connect talent across our organization, and every experience we design and execute includes talent from different functions and businesses across our portfolio of brands. The feedback we've received from talent is that our experiences help make the organization feel smaller, as connections are built with colleagues from across the portfolio.

What are the aims of bringing participants into Talent Labs?

There are multiple goals, depending on what type of Talent Lab experience someone is nominated and selected to attend. Experiences on our align track are designed to align talent that are new to the company or to a role that includes a significant shift (ie leading people for the first time, transitioning to being a manager of managers/functional leader, etc) to the expectations of that role, and important elements of the business and company culture that are relevant to them. Experiences on our *build* track build the core media skills, business acumen and capabilities needed to drive NBCUniversal's business priorities forward. On this track we've opted to focus on skills like digital literacy vs more traditional offerings like presentation skills – because that's what more critical for the organization. Experiences on our *accelerate* track challenge our top talent to be creative, invent, and deliver the future of media. This track is full of action learning experiences that bring great talent together to work on real challenges our company is facing.

How are participants selected?

Talent is selected through a nomination process that we partner with HR and business leaders on. For each experience, we have nomination criteria that help ensure we can select a cohort that is both diverse in the types of experience they have, but at a similar level in the organization so they can form relationships that are mutually beneficial.

How does the wider business benefit from their participation?

Since the Talent Lab launched in 2013, over 4,000 NBCUniversal employees across the globe have participated in one of our experiences.

Because we serve talent that have a great amount of impact across the organization, we see several elements impact the business outside of the lab. While we can't claim credit in its entirety, the Talent Lab has helped foster connections across our businesses, encourage collaboration, and spur innovation. We also consistently see higher levels of engagement from employees that participate in a Talent Lab experience, and for leaders that participate in Talent Lab experiences, we also see higher engagement scores for their teams.

How is it integrated with, or does it strengthen the organizations culture?

As we design our experiences, there are three things that are table stakes and must be integrated in the experience: driving our credo and values, executive sponsored (and not just in 'name' – true sponsorship with review of design, feedback and input, and support making connections within the organization), and driving our strategic priorities. By doing each of these elements in every experience, we ensure that smartly advancing our culture is at the heart of each experience. It looks different in each experience as well, as the impact you can have on our strategic priorities is different if you're a manager or a senior vice president – but wherever you are, we meet you with the message tailored to your level and experience.

How successful has the programme been?

We're very pleased with success of the Talent Lab (which is much bigger than a single programme – it's a true suite of programmes, that each invest several months in development). We've seen a tremendous number of our alumni promoted or moved into expanded roles. We've heard talent that were at a crossroads in their careers decide to stay at NBCUniversal in part because of an experience. And we can see and hear from our talent how we've impacted the culture of the company.

Is there anything else we should know?

Part of what is really the magic or 'secret sauce' for us, is leveraging our company's assets in ways that only we can. Our talent may hear from a head of production about a show's strategy on the show's set, experience the magic of our theme parks first hand, or talk about culture from the floor of one of our television studios in historic 30 Rockefeller Plaza – where you can see and feel our legacy and future at every turn. Don't just talk about it – show it whenever you can.

What are your top three tips for others who might want to create a programme that develops high-potential talent?

1 Bring the business into it – it has to be challenging and business relevant to participants. Leveraging real challenges that exist in the business is great for challenging your high-potential talent.

2 Timeliness is key, especially with business challenges. You can't reuse a challenge over and over for years as it will go stale. Your high-potential talent programmes should remain on the cutting edge if you want to remain relevant.

3 Spend the time to develop and nurture a cohort. What you can teach and bring into an experience is great, but helping your high-potential talent develop strong relationships with each other is just as valuable.

Multi-talented people

When we define people by their job title, we pigeonhole them. In the days where linear organizations required people to strip down their individuality and other capabilities to do a specific task repetitively, over and over, there may have been a value to that. But the world doesn't work like that anymore.

Organizations benefit when they create the opportunity for contribution and that may go beyond a specific qualification. If you keep people in a box, how will you know what they're capable of when they're unleashed?

Sally is a management accountant, but every weekend she spends hours engaged in her hobby of still-life photography. In a traditional organization, Sally's pursuits beyond the nine-to-five are irrelevant, as long as the accounts are done. When the marketing department needs some product photography done, it outsources to an external supplier, specializing in that skill.

In a human organization, Sally is part of the community, connected and recognized as a human. The fact that a member of the community who understands the brand has the capability to contribute more widely is a benefit internally, externally and saves a bit of cash too.

The more a person contributes as themselves, the more connected they are to an organization and the greater morale, productivity, output and other positive factors become. By focusing on who we are and everything we have to offer, our employers are able to plug into much more than basic tasks. Everyone benefits, it just requires the strategic ability to look beyond the traditional job title/job description combination and see people as part of the community, part of the story we create together.

Temper your enthusiasm though, freedom to contribute is one thing, but remember that freedom needs to fall within the parameters of the minimum viable structure. Everything still needs to be done!

Your way of doing things

The conversation on recruiting here may seem light on actual instruction. That's because it needs to be.

Every organization is different, so the way it builds its people strategy needs to be different. If you do what everyone else does, what will set you apart? Building a human workplace is as simple as focusing on people first and reaping the rewards. It offers a strategic direction built around ideas, but those ideas need to be applied to your own specific circumstances.

Understanding who the right people are allows you to build a strategy to understand where they are, which helps you go out and find them. Engaging them as part of the community and your wider network is the next step, so that when you need them, they are connected, in reach and can be brought down through the funnel.

Once you understand who your people are, you can go out and find them.

Keeping people

Drawing your people closer to the nucleus of your community as workers is a responsibility. The effort to get the right people requires you to keep them there. It's the strength of the connection that creates that.

If everyone has their own purpose that potentially influences them more powerfully than the business vision that the community aligns around, the organization needs to deliver one of two things – a coherent one-size-fits-all approach that caters for everyone, or an offering that allows the individuals to shape their own experience.

If there's value in unleashing everyone to be themselves and benefit in helping them to be the best version of that self within the community, the organization needs to cherish the individuals it has. It has to value its people above all else. That's not because they are assets, or commodities, or resources, or any other transactional thing, it's because they are its life-blood. Without people there is no organization – they are all about people.

This is where so many leaders go wrong. They assume that by constantly giving, they will encourage the right behaviours from their people.

A friend of mine is part of the leadership team of a small business. In conversation I mentioned freedom within parameters, to which she retold the countless pub lunches, summer ice creams, pub visits and away days that seemed to have no impact on performance. If anything, these perks had come to be expected and a stand-off was now developing between the people and the leaders.

This is not an equal relationship. A people-first workplace regards all people as of equal importance and the relationship must be two-way – adult. Applying freedoms without reinforcing the required parameters, produces something akin to a dysfunctional parent–child relationship. The framework around the relationship needs to be set, with a set of parameters linked to behaviours, as we saw in Buffer's case. If people are to take responsibility for their own actions, they need to be clear of the expectations and prepared to align their contribution with them, or leave the community.

To remain a part of the community, a person must respect the community parameters, guidelines or rules (however you want to define them), exhibit the behaviours and act in a way that's appropriate for the community. When those parameters are in place, this can happen and where it doesn't, the likelihood is that this is a person not aligned with the community. It's the wrong person.

A question of value

The shared vision is a strong social connector and the fundamental building blocks on which a strong organization is built. Even when a connection is strong, it still takes effort to keep your community together and functioning at its best. Expecting people to thrive just because they believe in the aims of your business is naive at best, arrogant at worst.

Traditionally, workers were expected to be grateful for a job and as the job valued their skills over their humanity, thriving wasn't a desired output – task completion was. Today though, we need ideas, innovation and collaboration and that requires people, real humans. They need to be nurtured.

If your organization is going to the effort of building an amazing community of people and bringing the right ones on a journey closer to its nucleus, it needs to benefit from that hard work and not just let it slide. To do that requires more hard work.

Allowing as much freedom as possible, setting the required parameters and structuring in the least formal way to ensure all this stays together is essential. The best example to learn from is perhaps a family unit. Compared with traditionally structured, complex organizations, the best functioning families are equally, if not more, effective, balancing these themes with an added level of care and connection. It's no surprise that businesses are starting to take the lead from family units.

Genuine human relationships

Families are based on human relationships, not transactions. In a family it matters who someone is, not just what they do. Their interests and qualities are nurtured to help them become the best version of themselves they possibly can be. Individuals in families give and take, they talk, they contribute. It's a dynamic that modern workplaces aspire to. It's the basis of the human workplace.

It's no surprise that many organizations are starting to adopt a 'family' approach to their people, helping them to thrive, connect and, as a natural result, stay as close as possible to the centre of the community and act as an external evangelist to engage others and bring them into the funnel of the organization.

Software development company Ustwo is a prime example. They regard their organization as a *Fampany* – a family that delivers the aims of the company. It creates a unique dynamic – a level of informality, mixed with a driven purpose. The personality of the Ustwo fampany is clear, but so is the dynamic. A simple look at their Tumblr blog shows a collection of images mixing achievement with affectionate teasing. It's a clear example of a community with a clear identity, set of behaviours, operating within parameters and focusing on the right people, in the right places, taking the right actions.

By setting the right parameters and confidently recruiting the right people, Ustwo is able to value those people in a whole new way. The old days of pay and bonus as a way of retaining and rewarding people are over. This mechanism is statistically proven to fail. It's transactional and today real connection beats transaction every time.

Valuing people as people reinforces the connection. It's a balance of thanking, trusting, listening and rewarding. It's about a wider connected contribution, rather than a two-way exchange.

How valued your people feel contributes heavily to the strength of your community and how much the people within it contribute. This is the real employee engagement. Give the people the right conditions to thrive and they will.

Setting boundaries

It's all about parameters though. Relentlessly throwing perks without setting boundaries is as destructive as doing nothing at all, maybe even more so. Without parameters, freedom becomes anarchy and anarchy is destructive.

Valuing people is about much more than surface shows of affection. The most effective families and communities are those with clearly defined parameters and expected behaviours that are valued and rewarded.

Valuing your people is about valuing their contribution as part of the community, not bowing down in thanks because they show up. It's a two-way thing. Contribution is exactly that and a condition of membership of the community. Effective organizations are based around relationships, not transactions and that takes careful planning.

The way you recognize and reward your people is a fundamental aspect of building the strength of your human workplace. It's the glue that bonds the connection and there are so many things you can do from day one, just make sure they align with (and reinforce) the business, its vision and behaviours. It's a family dynamic that does nothing more than allows your people to thrive. Getting it right takes work, strategy and constant effort.

Be warned – when families don't function, they break! When a family breaks it's destructive, but when people thrive, organizations thrive too.

CASE STUDY

Interview: Cesar Villa, director, total rewards, the Hershey Company

As director, total rewards at the Hershey Company, Cesar Villa is tasked with developing its reward and recognition philosophy, principles and strategy. Reflecting the roots of the organization, this approach has evolved to focus on more than purely rewards. Cesar shared with me Hershey's philosophy, why it works and how recognizing each other is a powerful reward in its own right.

With a global workforce of 18,000 employees across 24 countries, Hershey is a large organization and a well-known brand. Founded in 1894, it also has an identity and heritage developed over more than a century. Reflecting this in recognizing its people was a challenge, but as Cesar explains: 'Our founder Milton Hershey was a philanthropist who wanted to support the community and invested much in developing the local town. This legacy underpins Hershey's identity as an organization today. From these roots, it continues to build by investing in its people first.'

During an average year, Hershey's employees are invited to participate in a company-wide engagement survey. One of the topics this includes is reward and recognition.

The 2013 survey showed that reward and recognition was an area requiring attention. This allowed the organization to evaluate and review what it had in place. Upon review, Cesar discovered inconsistency and that not all employees were receiving the same experience of recognition by the company. Although a global budget was dedicated to reward, it was distributed locally by managers at their discretion.

During the internal recognition assessment, Hershey discovered that one area had created a programme of peer-to-peer recognition. This group had the highest level of satisfaction on rewards and recognition across the overall business, despite not investing the most in financial reward. This proved to the business that a consistent programme, focused on people-based recognition with small tokens of appreciation, could create more positive impact than traditional financial-first approaches.

Investigating this concept further, Cesar discovered that many leading organizations had adopted one coherent programme across their entire global business. With this proof of concept, he started looking at options for Hershey's approach, validated potential partners based on experience and expertise, before selecting Globoforce as their provider. This became the *Hershey Smiles* programme.

The simplicity of use, global platform and accessibility of the interface was an essential aspect in choosing the right recognition platform for Hershey. Offering an intuitive service that didn't require training or adaption to integrate into day-to-day behaviours and routines supported rapid, seamless adoption and made this effort truly about recognizing their people and the great work they do, rather than imposing a new and unfamiliar system that needed a huge effort to encourage participation.

Hershey's recognition goals

- Create one single, consistent global recognition philosophy and platform.
- Give the same experience to all employees in the organization.
- Develop a culture of recognition that increases leadership and engagement.
- Support Hershey as an employer of choice and best place to work.

The previous culture of recognition was top-down, with people awaiting recognition from managers, but this new global approach enabled recognition to happen on the spot, in the act, peer to peer, cross-team and cross-location. It allowed recognition to flow up, down and around the organization in any direction, creating positive impact.

Hershey's new recognition platform was linked to its organizational values, allowing them to become real behaviours:

- open to possibilities;
- growing together;
- one Hershey;
- making a difference.

When any of these values are seen manifesting in behaviour, they can be recognized, reinforcing them as real and helping to compile the Hershey story globally.

Hershey's three pillars compensation strategy

1 Reward: special compensation for high-impact achievements. Low in frequency/high in cost.
2 Recognition: day-to-day achievements aligned with company values. High in frequency/low in cost.
3 Appreciation: non-monetary items or events to engage employees.

To measure success in implementation, Hershey selected four different metrics:

1 individual recognition instances;
2 nominations;
3 overall recognition frequency;
4 overall satisfaction/engagement scores.

In the three years since the platform was launched, Hershey has seen a huge increase in recognition and measured engagement across its global workforce. This includes:

- over 73 per cent of 18,000 employees across 24 countries receiving at least one recognition;
- over 70 per cent of leaders sending a recognition and over 30 per cent for all employees;
- consistent increase in overall recognition frequency;
- 23 per cent increase in rewards and recognition satisfaction over three years as measured by the annual engagement survey;
- once every seven minutes a Hershey employee is recognized by a colleague.

The benefit to the organization of focusing on recognition has been huge. Impact can be created through the simplest of approaches – sometimes just saying thanks or well done can do much more than a financial reward alone ever could.

Thriving people

Organizations are platforms for people to thrive. When people thrive, the platform is effective and the business thrives too. Not only are organizations all about people, they are most effective when designed and delivered in a way that unleashes those people to be the best that they can be.

The best judge of what it takes to think best, work best, collaborate best and act best at any given time, is the individual, team or community itself. Given the right platform, the community can select the best way to work to achieve its goals.

Allowed to be amazing

Building organizations designed to do nothing more than enabling people to be their best, is a new idea. We're used to organizations dictating how we work, not providing options for us to choose from in piecing together our own version of great. Place, space, tools, structure – all of these things need to be available. Providing a kit of parts, from which every individual creates its ideal working conditions sounds like a bold and risky move, when in fact it's quite the opposite.

When people are unleashed to be amazing on their terms (within the parameters of the organization) their potential is unlocked. An environment that supports everyone in being their best, by providing the platform for it, transfers the responsibility for accessing that platform to the individual. It trusts the right people to do the right things, by creating the conditions for them to do it.

Unlocking people's potential in this way, strengthens the connection between workers and business, without tearing apart the shape or form of the organization. It can still be a triangle, as long as it allows work to be unleashed.

The rise of the six-hour working day in Sweden is a great example of this in action. With a third of employees distracted at work for up to three hours a day (*Daily Telegraph*, 2015), it's easy to understand how working two disciplined three-hour stints, with no distractions, separated by a communal lunch break and a zero-tolerance policy on working outside these hours, can support people in improving wellness and performance through defined parameters.

By setting a parameter and reinforcing the boundary between work and personal time, organizations who adopt this approach report many benefits. Increased free time away from work, more productive time at work and less distraction are all reported benefits. But as a dictatorial approach that needs to be enforced, can it ever be natural and can it move away from traditional distrust, control and presenteeism, to the trust, self-defined activity-based approach to work that really unleashes humans to be their best? Probably not.

This idea is great in a transitioning workplace where the lines between work and home have blurred, without balance or integration being achieved. It works where there's a risk of overworking, driving towards balance and achieving many benefits, but it doesn't offer true freedom. With working hours set strictly and enforced, it doesn't account outliers and variances. It's a one-size-fits-all approach, in a world where people increasingly expect to curate their own experience.

Buffer operates a global team, without operating a single physical office. It works hard to implement systems of communication and collaboration, fostering a tight and committed community. The connection is solid, as are the parameters – the level of activity expected by its people. Rather than the enforced 'balance' through strict working hours and associated rules of what can and can't be done at given times, or during 'work' hours seen in organizations implementing the six-hour work day, Buffer achieves a level of integration, where activity is undertaken as part of the individual's life, not separated from it. The resulting bond between the members of the community is very strong.

Both approaches allow people to truly thrive within the organizational community. To thrive completely in work, people need to be free to create the experience that suits them. They need the freedom to do the right things, in the right place and be provided with the toolkit to make that possible.

Employee experience

Just as business has talked about customer experience for decades, it's now realizing that, because people are people within the community, the experience workers have within the community is just as important in securing their contribution to success.

Successful platforms offer the right UX through a quality UI and that is now increasingly becoming the focus of the organization. It's not a question of managing resources and making sure they do what they're told, it's creating the platform for people to thrive, because when they do, the business does too.

Predictive analytics

It would be easy to assume that a human workplace should be anti-technology, but the reality is quite the opposite. Technology is proving to be the single most important enabler to all of this movement.

- Connectivity allows us to rethink where and how we work.
- Communication supports the flow of information anyway, anyhow, anywhere.
- Technology enables contribution and accountability, without being necessarily tied to specific places and times.

The rise of big data and with it, the ability to predict the wants, needs, likely actions and task requirements of workers (predictive analytics) is allowing organizations to fuel personalized experiences within the community that enables them to thrive at any time.

If the UI of the organization can understand enough about the worker to know what they may need in any given circumstance, it actively contributes to their positive experience – enabling them to work better. As with all aspects of creating a human workplace, the organization must provide the platform. Technology for the sake of technology is as pointless as anything else done for no reason, but when the right things are done for the right reason, the community functions at its best.

Using technology as an enabler that forms part of the employee experience and positively contributes to the community achieving its aims is the only way it should be approached and engaged. Anything else is overkill. If we go too far down the road of Big Brother watching our people's every move, we may as well continue to contract them to sit in a box and dictate what they do.

CASE STUDY

Interview: Theresa McHenry, senior human resources director, Microsoft UK

As a large global organization famous for its technology and data products and services, it would be easy to assume that Microsoft's focus would be on automation over humanity in the workplace. Theresa McHenry, senior human resources director took some time to discuss how tech and data can actually help create more human workplaces, how it's possible and what that looks like in an organization that operates in over 100 countries.

The work we're doing is not about defaulting to technology doing everything for you but using it as an enabler, understanding how to make work a more interactive, involved experience. Taking the natural way you would work, communicate and be, then enabling that through technology.

The ultimate goal is to create a personalized experience. Technology that knows who you are and what you need, creating that immersive connection at work so that you can be the best you can. What aspects of the workplace could be more technology enabled, that in turn allows us all to be more human?

As individuals, we all have different needs during the day. Rather than the organization prescribing how people will work, tech and data are enabling the organization to get out of the way and in turn, allowing people the space to do their best work as individuals, in their own way. Physical workplaces are required and won't ever disappear, because they provide the right space for work and opportunities for connections. Increasingly, people come to work less to complete tasks, more to meet and talk and share. The physical workplace is more of a place where people come to connect to the organization, than out of a need to get work done.

For a global organization like Microsoft, adopting these enabling ideas through its business is a combination of global strategy and local delivery. It ebbs and flows between local and global. Strategy, product, service and workflow decisions have a set of global principles, frameworks that outline what the organization is looking to deliver. It's a degree of global guidance, with an ability to decide locally how to best to make it work. There are market trends and competition in different locations that need to be considered. A broad local view of these factors allows for decisions to be made in the right context.

There's an increasingly strong overlap between business functions related to people. The creation of Microsoft's London office, a collaborative, flexible space, was the catalyst of this in the UK. Through this opportunity to bring people in different groups together, we also delivered a reinvestment in developing the workplace, all from a cost-neutral perspective. The combination of goals needed us to consider:

- Internal communications: goals for an environment where people can connect and communicate.
- Facilities management: delivering cost-effective services that support great work.
- Human resources: enabling people to be their best.
- Operations: delivering the work that needs to be done.

Effective, conversational change management binds these together. Change happens and happens for different reasons. On the business side, for example, a drive to save space or money. From an evolutionary perspective, technology is being adopted that changes the way people work. Even when a traditional business driver creates change, it's able to deliver wider benefits in helping to unlock people to do their best work.

Over recent years, Microsoft as an organization has changed, under a new CEO with a new vision. Adapting effectively to this has been enabled by a combination of buy-in to the vision, underpinned by authentic, clear leadership and enabled by a mindset shift across the organization.

This has created an empowering place to work, with opportunity for people to choose to be a part of it. Our challenge is how do we help people, even when their choice is to not be a part of it. Because that's OK, too.

For a company like Microsoft, technology is the enabler of all of this. In itself, it's not the end goal. It accelerates things, breaks silos faster, connects people faster. The way information flows up and down and around the organization has changed phenomenally and it allows the organization to behave in a flatter way. Leaders and employees are coming closer together via virtual proximity, without needing to completely restructure the organization.

You don't want to be constrained by your role. Who you are and experiences you bring means you can offer a breadth of insight and contribution, which creates more value for you and the organization. It's a case of tapping in to all the skill people have, beyond their job parameters, allowing them to participate more fully. Technology is allowing this to happen.

As an individual, it's so much more rewarding to play a full part, than just repeat tasks. When you connect people in a more networked way, they form groups around shared interests, making that expertise and insight available to the entire organization. These environments also make people far more interested in offering to help and support proactively.

From an HR perspective, we're looking at how to make technology work for Microsoft. It's easy to see benefits from a recruitment perspective, for example. Through interactive mediums like Sway, we're able to send candidates a more immersive amount of information on Microsoft and give them a rich perspective as part of their recruitment experience

It goes back to personalization and individualization. Packaging up information in a way that feels specific to that person and their needs from the experience or interaction with the organization. Giving people exactly the information they need, when they need it is essential. Artificial intelligence will help move this forward, but by knowing a person, their role, preferences and location, data can start to build the right experience by presenting them with information that enhances their day. Predictive analytics is powerful in many ways and can certainly to create a more human experience.

The possibilities ahead as technology develops are exciting!

Unleashing people

It is important to unleash humans, rather than turning humans into robots. Today, we have robots to do robotic jobs – we need to unleash humans to create impact in real ways:

- creativity;
- collaboration;
- communication;
- compassion.

These are all things that humans are amazing at. Coincidentally, they are all things our businesses need in order to thrive in the modern world.

If humans being humans bring real, tangible benefits to our organizations, the only way to harness that benefit is to unleash them to be just that.

Learning/teaching

If we're moving away from a focus on single-task working, then we need to focus on much more than traditional training. We've all spent times on mind-numbing courses that are required to prove we can do our jobs. The number of hours I spent in mandatory manual handling training, despite never working in a role that required me to lift more than a pen still makes me want to weep!

If our organizations are to unleash people, they need to develop those people as individuals, not as machines. In a community, humans that thrive contribute more – in short, better humans do better work. It's the organization's responsibility to enable that.

By moving the responsibility for development to the individual rather than a token effort by management to tick boxes on a training plan through an annual appraisal, a more connected, dynamic approach can be developed.

Today, we have a near limitless amount of information at our fingertips. By creating communities where information flows and individuals are empowered to utilize the platform in their own way to thrive in their work, trusting them to develop themselves, through constant conversation and feedback is effective.

Accessing the power of the community and our wider connected networks, working out loud so that our peers can suggest and enabling each of us to develop in our own way, rather than through a set of generic training, unleashes our people to better work.

Immersive experiences, encouraging behaviours, providing stimulus and open, honest conversation, drive these things. Just as our organizations are constantly evolving as they receive feedback from the users, so the users themselves evolve on their journey, through their interactions with others.

It's a dynamic, open system, designed to evolve. It just needs to be allowed to happen.

Leading people

Where the focus is on creating a platform for the right people, in the right places, to do the right thing, management no longer exists. The sole purpose of the leaders in an organization is to build that platform and ensure it's working at its best to enable its users to thrive in pursuit of their vision.

Rather than forcing workers to do certain things, leaders today (whether they realize it or not) are responsible for creating the UX. They're responsible for creating the right experience for every individual within the community to unleash them and allow them to do their very best work.

It's a coin flip.

Leaders today cannot be dictatorial and expect to succeed. Successful platform building comes from listening to user feedback, then providing the solutions to problems and meeting needs the user base has. In short, they must be human.

CASE STUDY

Interview: Chris Baréz-Brown

Chris Baréz-Brown is a speaker, author and founder of Upping Your Elvis. Inspired by Bono's question 'who's Elvis round here?', he helps organizations and their people bring energy and impact to everything they do. He shared some thoughts on unleashing Elvis with me.

The Elvis question essentially asks who here is a brand, or a maverick that gets stuff done? It's based on the knowledge that those who are have more energy about them and love doing what they do.

I personally believe that for an organization to win these days, we need everyone to find their inner Elvis. That means being more of yourself, knowing who you are and what you stand for, coming with more energy and passion, being able to self-express, trying things out and learning from them.

This can be done through focusing on leadership in two ways:

- Creative leadership: helping leaders become more creative, energetic and dynamic so they can wrestle the future better.
- Conscious leadership: enabling leaders to be in tune with themselves, the people they work with and the context of their business.

The two approaches go hand in hand, because without consciousness, people can't be creative.

Traditionally, organizations create barriers to creativity through imposing process and procedure. This is partly due to the psychology of organizations, where they become self-complicating. If you leave a room full of managers alone, they will naturally complicate things. By attempting to impose process and structure in the interests of efficiency, what actually happens is that things get tied in knots.

Because people have a role, function and a very specific focus around their remit, that's where the scope of their thinking focuses and they don't often consider the bigger picture – the overall system in which their role operates.

From the individual point of view, we all join jobs with energy and excitement, then we socialize with the norms and emulate the leaders. It's how people learn to get on and be accepted, right from our school days. A natural consequence of this is that we begin to lose touch with who we are and act in a way we think we're expected to.

When this happens we toughen up, start to act sensibly and disconnect our emotions from our work. On day one we all turn up keen and ready to change the world, but it's so easy to lose that as we socialize with the norms of the organization and people around us.

We need to step back from the busyness and the job titles and allow ourselves some leadership rehab, plug back into who we are, what makes us unique and what makes us tick. Because by doing that, we can re-energize and bring that passionate creativity back to our own work, as well as the organizations we work in.

For complex organizations to allow an element of humanity back into their work, enabling their people to show up and feel passionate, liberated and free to contribute, takes a conscious effort. It's achievable, but will never come from a process initiative or a new way of rewarding people.

There are things you can do to spark that off, but it also comes from leaders leading by example. If the leaders turn up passionate, excited and energized, that spreads through everyone else. If you have a load of people looking at numbers, doing nothing but worrying how they're going to report to the city, you'll get an organization that behaves in that way too.

To change behaviour you have to be more conscious. Otherwise you'll just continue to do what you've done before.

Five tips to introduce Elvis into your organization

1 Encourage experimentation every day.

2 Celebrate success and failure equally.

3 Learn from mistakes.

4 Constantly demand and provide feedback.

5 Be yourself.

Feedback

The annual appraisal is dead. Really, it's been redundant for years. Nothing more than a paper-pushing annual exercise to show that some effort has been made to manage a worker, it more often than not leads to a forced conversation and a list of actions that are ignored until the same torturous time next year.

The most difficult aspect of this, as well as the most welcome one, is the provision of feedback up the seniority chain, as well as down. It's traditionally unthinkable to question your manager and therein lies the problem. The idea of feedback in the workplace is generally seen as a negative thing. Tied into visions of formal appraisals and annual lists of how to improve, it's a mis-definition and a remnant of a more formal past – something which people-focused workplaces are eroding.

Just as design thinking allows products and organizations in perpetual beta to receive constant, ongoing (positive and negative) feedback, so it applies to the people in these communities. Every individual is in perpetual beta, seeking to develop and do their best work. Unless they receive the feedback from their own market (the workplace community), they will be unable to know how to develop, or the areas in which they're doing well.

Look at any common feedback platforms we use every day. TripAdvisor, Facebook, Amazon, Medium. Whether purchasing, experiencing, producing or conversing, we comment and expect comment as part of what fuels that community. In the community of a human workplace, feedback works in just the same way. It's part of recognition. Recognizing the contribution, successes and developmental needs of each individual, in order for them to participate fully in the community. When everyone is able to do that, the community benefits.

The question isn't whether you should be opening up feedback as a stand-ard part of the organizational conversation, but how to do it.

CASE STUDY

Creating a culture of feedback at MEC

MEC is one of the world's leading advertising and media planning agencies. Siobhan Brunwin, head of learning and development at MEC UK, is leading the company's mission to create a culture of feedback. She shared with me why this is important for MEC and, just as importantly, how they are integrating it into the global organization.

Establishing a culture of feedback is what everyone wants to do at the moment. Some organizations seem to have nailed it. In these places, two-way feedback has become the norm and there are great benefits to the organization. It takes time to get there and at MEC we have embarked on the journey with that as our goal. Our drive to achieve it came from an appraisal system that wasn't working.

No one has ever said, 'I'm really looking forward to my annual appraisal'. After conducting focus groups at all levels in the organization to understand in detail how well the annual appraisal system was working, we discovered that:

- people weren't getting value from the conversation;
- managers were finding the process stressful and an additional workload;
- the process seemed clunky and ineffective.

At MEC, we strive to create a forward-thinking, progressive culture. Operating an old-fashioned traditional appraisal and feedback programme was no longer aligning well with what we wanted to achieve as an organization. Two key problems with the annual appraisal were that it had become an excuse to put-off addressing issues and people also felt hesitant to ask for feedback during the rest of the year. It was blocking what it set out to achieve.

We went out to the market and discovered a number of tools available to help organizations do this better. We met with six software providers that were taking the formality out of the appraisal setting, performance management, feedback provision and trying to make it something that fits and flows into the organization.

MEC has approached feedback from two perspectives, the tech tool and culture. From a tool perspective, that has gone well, but from a culture perspective, it remains a work in progress and it will take a few years to get to the position where we can say we really have a true culture of recognition and feedback.

Adding that level of recognition is important, because too often feedback in organizations is seen as negative, outlining areas for improvement rather than recognizing what has been done well. A focus on recognition also moves the conversation away from being between only a direct manager and the employee. By enabling open feedback and recognition, it broadens the conversation. In the MEC business, people work across teams, across clients, in different locations and on different projects. Our aim is to enable cross-peer feedback that fits with such a dynamic organization.

This is the MEC people and culture team's first global project. From a UK perspective, the process was driven by consultation with our people – over 200 were engaged in the focus groups that shaped recommendations for the programme. We then started to spread the ideas globally, from a global strategy, local implementation perspective. The aim is to keep everything simple, taking feedback from a positive place. We believe that if you focus on the weakness you can create competence, but if you focus on the strengths you can create excellence. Even when developmental feedback is required, it's not perceived as negative. It means the person providing it cares enough to have that difficult conversation.

Reducing structure and removing formality, to make giving and receiving feedback a positive experience, is also a core part of the MEC approach and helps to remove negative perceptions around feedback. Rather than sitting across a table, going for a walk is encouraged, creating a real human connection and making the conversation easier. It's a powerful approach that creates impact for everyone.

Identifying when and how to provide feedback

- Where are the opportunities for feedback?
- How can it be given and received in a timely way?
- Can it be external (client) as well as internal (colleague)?

Already, across MEC there is a shift to more informal conversations, openness and requests for feedback and there is still work to be done. This is a constant evolution and we'll continue to refine the tools, as well as the cultural integration to ensure that the MEC culture of feedback continuously develops and benefits everyone.

Money

The M-word deserves some mention, because it has always been the driver at the heart of a business. The package has always been a draw in securing people to work for your organization, but we're now seeing data that shows it's not an effective way of securing the right people.

Studies show that employee happiness resulting from a pay action only lasts one to four weeks (Globoforce, 2016). While money, in the short-term can turn heads, it's fickle and doesn't create a true connection between people and organization. The stronger the connection, the stronger the community and while money is necessary as part of a fair reward package, it's no longer the key focus for many workers.

It's not a generational thing, it's just fact.

CASE STUDY

Perspective: Derek Irvine, executive vice president, strategy and consulting services, Globoforce

As one of the world's foremost experts on employee recognition and engagement, Derek helps business leaders set a higher vision and ambition for their company culture. He has worked with some of the most complex organizations on the planet, helping unlock them through the power of recognition and is co-author of The Power of Thanks.

It's all about creating a great place to work.

Driving that by creating a great employee experience is proven by data to be worthwhile. It starts with clarity of direction, staying mindful of what you've achieved and what you want to achieve. Helping all your people to understand that their work contributes to the company achieving its goals and explaining the role they each have to play in that is essential. So is celebrating that contribution.

Giving people a voice through feedback and conversation is one way to both enable and celebrate contribution. These things are all part of creating that great employee experience and from a business perspective, the return on investment on doing that is clear. At Globoforce, we focus on our internal employee experience and as a result, our measures of trust and engagement with the organization are consistently in the high 90s.

No one event, interaction or approach creates this momentum that lasts throughout the year. It's a question of consistency. Briefing – feedback, socializing, sharing, celebrating, recognizing – all these things contribute to the overall momentum of keeping the experience right. By doing this, it's possible to ensure that everyone has:

- colleagues that they know and trust;
- supportive friends in the workplace;
- clarity around their contribution;
- understanding of the impact their own actions create.

Financial income and psychological income both need to be present as part of that experience. It can't be only about the transactional financial exchange of hours for money. If you focus only on financial reward, it becomes an inappropriately balanced deal and, although it might last for a while, it will eventually break. When it does, attracting, retaining and engaging people becomes difficult.

Organizations are waking up to this new reality, because employees are demanding it. Because of the amount of time people spend in work, their understanding of work and their expectations from it are modernizing.

Meeting these demands sounds like a challenge, but for corporate leaders it's a win-win situation, because if you get that balance right, the bottom line benefits. Good people, a strong culture, balance and readiness to contribute and succeed can only be a good thing for any organization. Those organizations which don't develop a strong employee experience run the risk of becoming irrelevant.

This change in expectation also requires a change in how organizations motivate people. Annual reviews and one-off annual bonuses are now shown to be ineffective, but for years were fundamental pillars of the transactional relationship between people and organizations. Employees are now asking for a more continuous conversation, continuous feedback and continuous compensation related to contribution.

These transactions are being replaced with conversation-oriented mechanisms to support performance management. Constant check-ins, quick feedback, relevant compensation are all effective and becoming more and more expected by workers.

A well-resourced social recognition programme tracks achievement, success and contribution. It's driven by colleagues and acts as a non-financial form of continuous pay. It has a greater impact on employee satisfaction and productivity throughout the year, yet costs a fraction of an annual bonus.

By fostering these human connections, conversation comes back into the workplace. It's less formal, less hierarchical and makes authentic, valuable human interactions. We're moving into a time where the obvious wake-up call for all organizations is understanding how technology can be used to aid human elements to come back into our work, for the benefit of everyone.

Connecting people peer to peer, at all levels of an organization, in all locations allows the organization to learn and gain the information it needs to adapt and succeed. Allowing that to happen in a frictionless, smooth way is essential. It's also simple.

Not all managers are comfortable with this shift, because their fundamental role is changing from one of control, to one of emotional understanding and communication. It's no longer about making sure people do set tasks, but creating an environment to empower people to take on tasks successfully and in their own way.

Managers are becoming coaches and experience enablers. Not all managers are comfortable with that, but technology can become an enabler for these core human skills. It can prompt and encourage behaviour, offer tips and reminders.

In a human workplace, everyone is able to be who they are. They come to work as themselves, not as someone else and, as a result, they can offer their best day's work to the organization.

These people feel appreciated, recognized, understand the direct impact of their work and know that it's meaningful. There are amazing statistics emerging, correlating employees who receive recognition for their contribution and organizational benefits. Typically, we're seeing that recognized employees are 50 per cent more likely to remain with the organization, with 32 per cent improvement in overall levels of engagement.

This isn't just a soft topic, these are significant figures from major organizations and compelling reasons to act.

Take your pick

It's down to your organization to select the right solutions that builds its platform. Providing the most effective kit of parts to deliver your organizational platform is the real challenge for our modern business leaders.

There is no model, or set of rules. Because your organization and its users is individual, the way you build it must be too. Taking ideas from other is great, but they can never be applied completely – everything must be adapted to your own context to be effective.

Just do the right things, for the right reasons.

Ten key ideas on people

1   The right person is far better than just any person.

2   Personal purpose comes before business purpose.

3   Individuality through diversity creates an advantage.

4   Encouraging real behaviours creates more impact than just defining values.

5   Contribution does much more for a business that attendance ever can.

6   Recruit for who someone is, not what they've done.

7   People have more to offer than the list of tasks on their job description.

8   Everyone works best when they can choose their preferred way to get things done.

9   Simple recognition can be more powerful than financial reward.

10   When people thrive, organizations do too.

Once an organization identifies who the right people are, it's able to start building a platform that enables them to thrive. That starts with creating the environment for their best work.

Task 4: defining behaviours

Rather than listing tokenistic values for your organization to stencil onto walls, identify a set of behaviours that everyone in the organization should role model. It will help define:

- who the right people are for your organization;
- how they connect with the business;
- the actions they take individually and collectively;
- the individual personality of your organization.

List 5–10 real behaviours, then start to think about how they can become a real part of your organizational platform.

References

Chapman, D telling the Buffer Story at All About People 2016 is available here: www.youtube.com/watch?v=GDtxRQVhsCs.

Globoforce (2016) 'Annual bonus, annual waste?' Available from www.globoforce. com/libraries/downloading-ebook-annual/ [Accessed 17 April 2017].

Hope, K (2016) 'Sleep deprivation "costs UK £40bn a year"', bbc.co.uk, 30 November. Available from: www.bbc.co.uk/news/business-38151180 [Accessed 17 April 2017].

HSE, Labour Force Survey (LFS) (2016). Available from: www.hse.gov.uk/statistics/ causdis/stress/ [Accessed 17 April 2017].

Huth, S (2015) 'Employees waste 759 hours each year due to workplace distractions', Telegraph.co.uk, 22 June. Available from: www.telegraph. co.uk/finance/jobs/11691728/Employees-waste-759-hours-each-year-due-to- workplace-distractions.html [Accessed 17 April 2017].

Lewis, G (2015) 'Third of employers see growth in presenteeism', CIPD reveals, 12 October. Available from: www2.cipd.co.uk/pm/peoplemanagement/b/ weblog/archive/2015/10/12/third-of-employers-see-growth-in-presenteeism-cipd- reveals-160.aspx [Accessed 17 April 2017].

McDougall, K speaking at All About People 2016 is available here: https://youtu. be/yQsuevxeOLg.

Mann, A and Harter, J (2016), 'The worldwide employee engagement crisis', Gallup, 7 January. Available from: www.gallup.com/businessjournal/188033/ worldwide-employee-engagement-crisis.aspx [Accessed 17 April 2017].

In all the right places   04

If an organization is working hard to make sure it finds and keeps the right people, making sure they're provided with the right place to thrive is equally important. Unless humans are provided the right conditions to thrive, they won't. Trying to concentrate at the kitchen table when there's a kids' party happening in your house is as impossible as trying to make ice cubes in an oven. Without the right environment or place, any type of work is impossible. Beyond that, thriving as a human is about much more than just working.

This chapter explores:

- workplace as an organization's clubhouse;
- the benefits of creating an amazing workplace;
- how design should start with people and evidence;
- the constant evolution of every workplace;
- why getting the basics right is the most important starting point.

A few thoughts on place

Let's not make the mistake of assuming that the only places where work happens are physical ones. Many of us now spend a lot of our working time in digital, virtual spaces which contribute equally to our working environment. While we may physically be somewhere, our actual work may be happening in a place that doesn't actually exist.

Social media sharing tool Buffer's team collaborates globally without setting foot in the same physical place on a day-to-day basis, because they have created the virtual environment that enables their people to thrive. Relying on technology to keep them connective and collaborative, they use a clear set of behaviours, expectations and parameters to maintain the right working environment, despite not being in the same room. There are tools, technologies and capabilities that mean our work happens anywhere it can happen. It can be integrated into our lives, rather than separated from them.

With an internet connection, a certain kind of worker can be just as effective on a train as in the centre of an office. The rise of virtual places for us to work has afforded us a new level of choice. Our work has simultaneously become more and less connected to the physical spaces we work in as a result.

Where work can happen

On one hand, some types of work can happen anywhere. On the other, because we have that flexibility, workers are now empowered to choose the best location for their work at any given time, so the physical workplace has had to up its game. To get your people to come to you when they don't need to, you must make them *want* to.

Of course, this 100 per cent freedom to work anywhere doesn't apply to all types of work. Mass manufacture has to happen where the machines are, nurses have to be where the patients and the equipment are, builders have to build on a building site, yet still elements of their work can be unleashed from specific physical environments. Due to the enabling influence of technology, manufacturing compliance analysis doesn't have to happen on the factory floor, healthcare doesn't have to be in a hospital, invoicing and planning doesn't need to be done in an office. It's freedom, within parameters.

Technology has given almost all types of worker the potential to choose where to undertake certain tasks and that's a huge reversal. WiFi, cloud and mobile computing has made most administrative work potentially mobile. Communications advances mean conversations can happen anywhere, without being tethered to a single location. In almost every industry, some element of work has been unleashed by technology.

Previously, the workplace was the de facto place for work. Now the organization needs to give its workers the right places to take the right actions, or they will choose to be elsewhere. Doing that is an integral part of its operation as a platform.

Because technology is enabling us to work differently, as users we're starting to expect that choice. If on any given day my best work can happen in a specific location or setting, it's surely in the organization's interest to unleash me to do that. The worker with the right tools, in the right place, does the best work.

The organization's responsibility is to provide the right people with the right places to help them to take the right actions, in pursuit of the business' aims. Because every organization is unique, the right place is as personal to it as the right people – understanding what it needs to be and how to create it is the trick!

Physical user interface/user experience

We've already established that every organization is a platform. It forms the *user interface* (UI) that drives the *user experience* (UX). The physical or virtual workplaces and locations it provides are the manifestation of that – the touchpoints between businesses and their people.

If that's the case, then the physical places an organization provides (if it chooses to provide them), driven by the virtual places where work can happen, are curated experiences. They are designed rather than de facto.

Let's call them *workplaces*.

In the pre-digital, pre-choice era, because people had to work in a certain place at a certain time, actually going to work was compulsory, there was no choice involved. Control was with the organization and physical workplaces were designed for that – they were designed so people could be micro-managed.

Sometimes, because the organization could see no value in doing anything more than providing its people somewhere, anywhere to work, workplaces were not designed at all. This was constricting. Shoehorning desks or machines into cheap commercial (or completely unsuitable) space is no way to unleash people to do their best work and some (but by no means all) organizations are starting to realize that.

Although the tide has been changing for decades, there are still workplaces designed around the philosophy of control and the notion that people *have* to come to work to play their full part. That's no longer necessarily the case.

The UI and UX of an app have to give people reason to use it. An organization needs to give people a reason to align with a purpose, or to use its platform. The workplace, as the physical manifestation of the organizational platform, is an extension of that. It needs to give people a reason to work there.

Unless it unleashes them to do their best work, or gives them another reason to be present, why would they choose to go there? Moreover, why would a business expect its people to be somewhere that wasn't unleashing them to do their best day's work?

The human experience

A 2014 study by the University of Warwick discovered that happy employees are 12 per cent more productive, while unhappy workers are 10 per cent less productive than the average (Oswald, Proto, Sgroi, 2014). It makes logical sense that a working environment should create that impact on the people who work there.

When I asked Neil Usher, purveyor of the *Workessence* workplace blog and then director of workplace at Sky, how he would define a human workplace, his response was:

> Perhaps a more interesting question is why a space intended to be inhabited by human beings wouldn't be conceived as a human workplace.

The use of the word *inhabit* is an interesting and fundamental one. Because we can now work from home (or anywhere else), we need to be at home at work. We need to be able to have the optimum experience that enables and actively supports us to do our best work at any given time, in a world where defined hours are being eroded fast.

Human workplaces are places that enable people to thrive. When people thrive, organizations thrive too. This is the most powerful reason why the actual place where people come to align with the organization matters. It's their touchpoint with the platform. It's where the connection between people and organization is strongest.

It's the home of the community.

Workplace as a clubhouse

Every strong community has a central meeting place that performs a function. It's where the community congregates to do what it does, in the most connected way. It's where the bond is most powerful. Thinking of the workplace in this way creates a new dynamic. Clubhouses aren't places of transaction, they are places of belonging. Far from a location purely to exchange hours for time, modern workplaces need to facilitate work and emphasize the connection between people and business. They need to make people *want* to be there and provide a benefit in that.

This benefit can be increased through enhancing collaboration, creating a more intense connection, fostering a sense of belonging, providing better opportunities for productivity, creating choice, offering social connections, or any other way a workplace can create the right UX for its specific community. For the workplace to act as an effective enabler for the organization it needs to foster a mix of services that fits what the business needs to achieve and the settings that create the conditions for its people as individuals and teams to achieve this.

Just as it's impossible to create a one-size-fits-all approach to building an organization, the same can be said for creating an amazing workplace. Look on it as a private members' club – a collection of people based around a shared purpose. They don't need to be in the same physical place to be part of that community, but when they are they receive direct access to services, environment and opportunities that they wouldn't get outside the clubhouse.

The benefits of a location with such a strong identity are clear. When people thrive, organizations thrive too. All the workplace needs to do is provide the place for that to happen. *It's simple, yet we make it so complicated!*

Intensity of connection

Inside the stadium

When you support a sports team, you're part of a dispersed community that congregates around that team. The connection is strongest in the team's home stadium.

The team itself is the nucleus of the community, the supporters in the stadium are where the community is at its most connected. Just because others aren't in the stadium, it doesn't mean they aren't part of the community though.

There are those congregating to watch on screens in bars, then there are those watching at home. Some passively listen to the game on the radio as they go about other things, others check the scores online the next morning and some pick up results out of passing interest only when they are in front of them.

The team's community radiates out in strength and intensity from the nucleus, yet even those who take the most passive interest by consuming messages around the team form part of that community. They all play a part and it's the sum of these parts that make up the community in its entirety.

Different locations, same purpose

This principle applies to organizations. The community can be dispersed, congregate in different locations and on their own terms to contribute to get behind the ultimate goal of the team, but each needs the right platform to contribute in their own way. Organizations provide their communities with this platform in the form of (physical) place, (virtual) space, tools, technology and communication. Workplace is that physical place for the community.

The stadium is where people flock – they gravitate towards it as the epicentre of the movement. Call it a head office, call it a clubhouse, the flagship location is where the good stuff happens. This is where the nucleus is, where the connected experience is at its most intense. It carries the team (business/brand) colours and represents the team in every aspect of its construction. It's the central focus of the community, designed to help the team and its supporters be their best in pursuit of helping the team win. There are a range of services it needs to provide to make that happen – services that go way deeper than aesthetics.

Beyond the flagship location, other locations are often needed to provide the level of connection the community needs. Clubhouse workplaces provide the next most intense connection, fully branded and designed for the community experience, in the context of local cultural nuances.

The larger the reach of the community, the more diverse these need to be. Across geographical and cultural borders, they need to provide a connection that supports contribution. These smaller locations still need to provide a recognizable, useful experience that allows the people in them to do the right things in pursuit of the collective vision.

Then there are those who are even more dispersed. Those working or supporting from home, who still need to contribute in their own way.

Whether stadium, clubhouse or remote experience, the challenge of creating a physical workplace isn't as simple as finding a building big enough to throw some desks in. It's a strategic manifestation of the organizational platform, tasked to unleash everyone involved to be their best – whatever role they may play.

The dispersed and interconnected workplaces each fit their position in terms of requirement, based on proximity to the community (see Figure 4.1).

Every workplace however large or small, connected or dispersed, needs to be part of the community, part of the organizational platform. It needs to provide that connection between people and business, unleashing everyone to do their best work.

If you build it, they will come. You just need to build it right!

Figure 4.1   Dispersed and interconnected workplaces

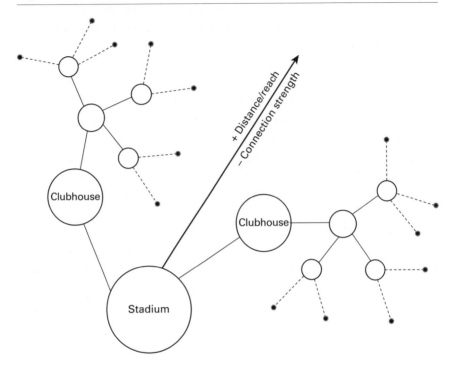

CASE STUDY

Interview: Sudhir Saseedharan, design manager, global design and engagement, corporate facilities, the LEGO Group

As the design manager in global design and engagement, Sudhir Saseedharan takes lead responsibility on a number of key LEGO workplace projects, including the London Hub and Shanghai Hub. Implementing a New Ways of Working approach requires a focus on flow, engagement and empowering the employees to make meaningful choices to work effectively, creating a different perspective on workplace design. He shared insights on the approach with me.

The reason for an organization having its own workplace design team is to understand what the core of what employees do and how design can be user-centric. Partly it's around attracting and retaining the best talent, but it's also to enable every employee do their best work. Engaged, motivated and satisfied employees are what helps propel the organization to the next level. In creating the physical working environment, we're trying to engage the employee in as many ways as possible – with the brand, with the workplace, with the team, with oneself.

To create an awesome, world-class workplace requires multiple levels of end-user engagement to access the right data to inform design. Our approach to engagement focuses on three groups, to gain insight into how the workplace affects different groups and different aspects of the organization.

Stakeholders
How can it be engaging keeping the overarching values of the LEGO Group in mind? Combining local relevance with global identity.

Employees
What do you need from physical, virtual and behavioural environment to succeed in your work?

Operational
How can the design help operations (everything begins after move-in)?

At the LEGO Group, the New Ways of Working (NWOW) approach is divided into physical, virtual and behavioural categories. NWOW has a set of guiding principles and each is interpreted for each of these categories. For example, if exploring how to create a feeling of connectedness, from a physical perspective we'd explore how to integrate LEGO history and branding into the workplace, alongside ways to create inspiring environments that trigger curiosity. We'd also look at how to bring different parts of the business into that environment so that all employees could understand the end-to-end process of the business.

The physical workplaces that are created in this way unleash the strategic aims set out by the NWOW guiding principles. In turn, these workplaces have a very big impact on the people who work in them. Firstly, they change the method of working from traditional, where you have your own desk, to a space where you have the opportunity to choose how to work. It's a big step, which makes the change process very important from the start.

Another shift is the move to collaboration, across departments. It breaks silos and allows employees to understand what others are doing, purely because of the proximity to each other. That helps everyone to understand the wider organizational picture. Everyone feels part of something bigger and that provides a sense of empowerment. This is all achieved by creating the right physical environment. In addition, the open dialogues and new interactions this kind of workplace creates, drive a different mindset, helping personal development and feeding new thinking.

Creating a recognizable global approach based on NWOW principles, then using end-user engagement to shape that for local delivery, allows for local cultural sensitivities and requirements. Global functional standards don't change, what does change is the local elements. We need to reflect the environment in which the workplace is created, as well as local rules, norms and laws. Lifestyle is also a factor. There are many things we take into account when creating workplaces and local relevance is one of the most important.

These ideas aren't just for office spaces. At the LEGO Group we have three kinds of workplaces:

- sales offices;
- hubs;
- manufacturing sites.

The Shanghai Hub is a flagship project. It took learnings from previous implementations in London and Singapore, while also having a strong local relevance. We had to emphasize on China and the local relevance which is more defined and less of a multi-cultural demographic compared to London and Singapore. Up until now, this is the most optimum example, but we know the next project will be even better.

No project is ever perfect, there are always things you could do better. But by taking those learnings through to the next project, you can consider these factors in the planning stage. There's also the perspective from user feedback. Post-occupancy evaluation from users once they are in the workplace, helps us to understand how well different aspects are working. This all informs the refinement of the project and inception of the next one. Every project is an 'employee first' experience.

Your people-first workplace: starting point

To create a workplace of any type that enables people to make their best contribution, Sudhir recommends these explorations:

- *Vision.* Start with the organization's values. What does it need to achieve?
- *Engagement.* Talk to employees. What is their idea of an ideal workplace?

Use these to drive the design and provision of any workplace.

Working from home

Back in 2013, incoming CEO of Yahoo! Marissa Meyer caused huge debate on home working by recalling all of the organization's people to work in offices. The view was that in the interests of communication and collaboration, everyone needed to be physically present and working side by side.

The secret to good working is being able to do your best work. To do that, you need to be in the place that enables you to do it, with the right tools for the job. That could be at home, just as much as it could be in any other location.

Not only do tasks vary, but other influences mean that the same person may be at their best in a different setting or location from one day to the next. When a team player needs to ideate, update or explore, then an office may be the best location, but when they need to think, do some admin, collect the kids from school, or change pace to avoid burnout, then home may suit better that day.

Giving people the responsibility for their own work is essential. Providing them with the flexibility to be or go wherever they need to be their best is the responsibility of the organization as an enabling platform.

Creating a physical workplace that offers benefits to being there, will make workers *want* to be there. Providing them with as much flexibility as possible around how, where and when they can work (freedom within parameters) will allow them to take responsibility for their best work at all times.

If someone works well on Sunday afternoons and less so on Thursday mornings, as long as the parameters of their work allow the exchange, why shouldn't it happen? Equally, if a worker can be their best at home, rather than in a custom-built workplace on a specific day, then there's no reason why they should be anywhere other than the place they can work best.

Sometimes we do our best work in our pyjamas at the kitchen table – if the parameters of the work allow, the organizational platform should always encourage it. By enabling this, the organization's workplace extends beyond the physical walls of its offices or factories. It's part of a service that the organization gives to its people. The service of the right place to enable them to take the right actions.

Creating the right experiences for our workers is essential. The closer we can get to offering them self-service work, built around their personal needs in a way that allows them to make their best contribution to the community, the better. If this experience can be enhanced through building their own stadium or clubhouse, then the stadium or clubhouse should be built. If, however, virtual connection is more prudent, then that should be fostered.

In reality, for most organizations, it will be a combination of the two. Physical place and virtual space contribute to enable people to do their best work. At home, in the designated workplace, on the moon, the only essential is that they are enabled to do it.

Being part of something

There are two things that a physical workplace is particularly well-placed to foster: 1) maintaining the connection between people and business that enables them to do their best work; and 2) fostering the collective identity by creating a sense of belonging.

By providing the most intense, immersive experience possible for all people, the workplace in the broadest sense can provide this. People-first organizations are enablers rather than controllers, and in order to enable, the experience people receive is essential. Positive experience enhances connection, and strong connection makes the community around the business more coherent.

The more coherent a community is, the better it functions. The physical workplace acts with the virtual tech and comms that bind the community in and around it to create the right experience. That experience needs to:

- reflect the shared vision;
- drive the right behaviours;
- enable best work;
- enhance the connection between people and business;
- create the conditions for the business and its people to thrive;
- unleash everyone through freedom within parameters.

For this to happen, not only does the workplace need to embody the best of the collective identity, it needs to recognize that, as individuals, people work in different ways at different times. Our best work is not a linear thing, it's a dynamic thing that changes daily. The conditions that best support my contribution today may be the same ones that block what I need to do tomorrow. Equally, what helps one person to work well, may prevent another from doing so.

CASE STUDY

Interview, Peter Baumann, SAP

Peter is SAP's global real estate and facilities head of projects EMEA. In recent times he has been responsible for delivering a number of large-scale workplace change projects across the region and continues to work on creating and launching new working environments for the organization.

In conversation, Peter shared his approach to not only informing great workplace design, but also driving the positive adoption that secures the investment in such projects.

At SAP, facilities management is changing from a service provider to the organization to an entity that understands the value proposition its work can bring to the entire company. By supporting the organizational structure and strategy, facilities management (FM) can simultaneously spread themes from the top-down and bottom-up, helping SAP to retain its legacy while driving its aims to become the cloud company of the future.

Peter identifies the approach he employs to delivering workplaces as being *with the people, for the people.*

Designing workplaces for the sake of a news story or some nice architectural pieces (even though these things will happen as a result of good design!), is the wrong reason. Workplaces exist to support the organization and its people in doing their best work.

He says 'It's essential to take the people along on the journey to the end result. We could deliver an office that looks nice, but without having involved the people, they might not adopt the new space or workstyle and we would not get to such a successful result.'

For Peter and SAP, it's elemental that the people are part of the success of a workplace. Including them in the design and delivery process is time consuming and requires tremendous effort, but when it's done in the right way the result is outrageous in terms of the level of adoption and positivity.

It drives the organization forward and in doing so, provides FM and the provision of working environments at SAP with a new level of recognition. SAP's workplace projects are driving the value proposition of the new organization.

Peter sees the emergence over time of a chief living officer role, where the connection between people, place and work is far more central to the organization than a service-focused FM department that reports to the chief finance officer.

This will bring a number of advantages, not least in ensuring the organization is able to find and keep the right people. Talent has won the war and today employers like SAP need to find competitive advantages to attract and retain the best people. The provision of a workplace that connects people with the purpose and identity of the organization, while enabling them to do their best work is a major part of that. At SAP, the physical workplace today is increasingly a platform of culture, collaboration and people.

For a workplace professional like Peter, being part of this shift is an exciting time. A decade ago organizations built offices and maintained spaces. Today workplace provides the basic platform for the organization and its people to realize their innovation and achieve their goals. Organizations like SAP are changing and moving forward. It's an amazing time for their evolving FM and workplace teams to be driving that through the working environment.

A major part of delivering an amazing, successful workplace is connecting it with people, and for that Peter has developed a change management approach that works. This approach engages people, creating the basis of common thinking while retaining individual local cultures, within the One SAP family. By adopting this approach, the business takes a huge benefit from workplace evolution. The successes of the projects prove the return on investment of taking the time to engage the people in the journey. Demonstrating the return on investment proves to the business that this approach is the best thing to continue doing. It's a question of leading the entire business through the journey, through a process of *influence without imposition*:

- Instead of imposing, bring people on the journey to the result.
- Show people why this idea is the best.
- Allow them to recognize and discover the answers for themselves.

You can't take 2,000 people through a workshop, but by taking 50–60 people through the journey, they adopt and defend the position, becoming ambassadors throughout the whole organization. They explain their experience and share it with anyone who has questions and issues.

Change management is engaged as part of the overall process, because SAP take people on the journey from the start and allow them to discover the answers first-hand, rather than have them imposed.

Peter likens the approach to surfing a wave:

Once you create the momentum around a project, ride it until the end. Don't give up. Keep doing what you do and that will create a fantastic result. Deliver workplace projects with the people, for the people.

This approach isn't a case of act now, apologize later. It's more collaborative process, because everyone comes on the journey from the start. Everyone learns on the journey, including those delivering the project. It's all based on insight.

First, understand the *why* of the entire project:

- brand;
- value;
- culture/identification;
- defining success (project and organization).

Once you have it, use this as the thread for your resulting explorations.

It's not purely about communicating detail, it's about taking the thread of the *why* and combining it with the *what* and *how* of great work. People aren't interested in cabling and desk size, they need the conceptual experience.

Peter's advice to other organizations looking to develop their own approach to delivering workplaces and connecting people with them is:

Tell the truth
Don't fear the conflict. Go for the resistance and communicate with it. Understand the real reason behind it, because then you can address it.

Address what people need, rather than what they think they want
Conflict is friction and friction creates heat. Heat is good – no one wants to freeze!

Places for people

As Neil Usher asserted, if a workplace is a space intended to be inhabited by human beings, why wouldn't it be conceived as a human workplace – created with them in mind?

In Neil's view, people-first being the design standard for all workplaces is prevented by a focus on efficiency rather than effectiveness. Focusing on how many people you can fit into a space, rather than looking at how effective the space is and how it enables people to do their jobs is a focus on short-term and indicative of an old-fashioned linear mindset.

Of course, spending less money on kitting out a workplace, or saving money today by fitting more people into a workplace regardless of the impact on their ability to work may seem prudent, but if people are unable to be their best, the organizational platform fails because by not providing the right place, it then actively blocks the right actions. Regardless of whether your organization has 100 per cent of the right people in place, if the workplace (or any other aspect of the platform) prevents them from doing great work, it actively blocks success.

Over recent years, Sky has evolved its workplaces into a series of locations designed to unleash people. At its Osterley Campus, buildings surround Sky Central – a landmark building where the right workspaces and settings are provided for everyone to thrive. The wider environment offers more interconnection between home and work life – a gym, a hairdressing salon, a small supermarket, outdoor spaces, social spaces and more. This is the stadium. In Leeds Dock, Sky's tech teams are unleashed in a progressive home that enables their work and personal lives in equal measure. This is one of Sky's clubhouses.

All of these spaces are recognizably Sky, providing a level of brand experience on a par with that received by customers. In fact, Sky's collective workplaces are designed to connect people with the Sky community and unleash them as individuals, rather than control them. The people are the customers of the workplace and it provides them with a set of services that gives each individual the ability to do their best work.

Understanding why any organization should be creating its workplaces people-first is simple and the same as the reason for building the organization around people in the first place. Neil summed it up perfectly, so we'll give him the last word on this:

> The only reason to create a world class workplace is so that people can do world class work.

In a human workplace, the investment in real estate is secondary to the investment in people – and rightly so. *A great building alone cannot secure your future, the right people doing the right things can.*

What they look like

Places for people have to enable them to thrive. For a person to really thrive it takes much more than just work. We thrive when we're well, satisfied, connected, when we're allowed to be human. Yes we need different spaces to work in different ways, but we also need spaces to relax, socialize, integrate aspects of our non-work life (eg exercise, shopping) and to generally do the things that in turn allow us to contribute our whole selves at work.

Designing on evidence

Workplace strategy as a discipline has seen a huge rise in popularity over recent years, as organizations come to realize that creating the right space for their people is about more than a coat of paint and new desks. It takes thoughtful design. To design thoughtfully, you need a starting point. Unbridled creativity has its value, but when its aimless, it can be destructive.

Traditional thinking on creativity associates it with abstract thought, and while there's no doubt that the best workplaces reframe the relationship between people, place and organization through new perspectives and re-imagined spaces, the complete freedom to design at random has to be within that parameter of helping people do their best work. A great workplace is an investment in space and an investment in people, in equal parts. A pretty workplace in which people are unable to be their best is no use at all.

The only brief is to design a place for people that connects them to the business and enables them to be their best, then add the aesthetic touches that will inspire them to new levels of creativity and innovation in their work. Getting to that people-first position requires a much wider viewpoint than a floor plan and understanding of square footage. It needs an in-depth knowledge of the business, its work, its people and the organizational platform that drives the community.

It needs to ask the right questions and use the right techniques to answer them. Questions like:

- Who is the company?
- What does it do?
- What does it want to do?
- Who are these people?
- How do they behave?
- How do they want to behave?
- How do they work?
- How could they work?
- What do they need to be their best?
- How can this be unlocked?
- How do they use space now?
- How could they use space better?
- What would inspire them?
- How can we create better?

Once gathered, this data can be utilized to inform amazing people-first design and create amazing workplaces that are truly fit for purpose. When whoever is tasked with designing your workspace has this information to guide them, they have the right parameters to work within. It creates the necessary focus, to create considered spaces – designed for a purpose, designed for people.

It's impossible to be exacting in design without the right amount and accuracy of information. Gathering the data is a challenge in its own right, too. Common approaches include staff interviews, surveys, on-site data gathering, space utilization studies and more. These manual methods are increasingly being supplemented by technology. Motion, heat and light sensors, beacons, bluetooth connectors and other tech are enabling the dynamic and constant collection of data that helps to answer the right questions and inform the design process.

Keep on designing

Because technology and the way we work is constantly changing, workplace design is a constant evolution. No workplace is ever truly finished. Like the organizations they serve, amazing workplaces are a perpetual work in progress.

Maintaining the Golden Gate Bridge in San Francisco takes constant work from a dedicated team, because as soon as each dab of paint is dry and exposed to the elements, the world starts to attack it. Without ongoing maintenance, the bridge would eventually rust and fail. The elements that attack and influence our organizations, changing the way people work and the way they need to work, also keep our workplaces evolving. Just as our organizations and our approach to work are adopting design thinking as their default setting, the workplace as part of the platform needs to do the same, or risk becoming quickly outmoded. The provision of a great workplace is a subscription service, not a one-off investment.

The questions that provide the data to inform workplace design are not just up-front queries. Once your workplace is built and operational, they need to be asked again and again. First to see that the workplace is delivering what it needs to, then repeated to make sure it continues to do so. The workplace industry calls this post-occupancy evaluation. The rest of us can call it design thinking. Neil Usher explored this 'perpetual beta workplace' idea, with reference to Brian Condon (Workessence blog, 2012).

Gather the data to *understand* what your workplace needs to deliver, *think* about what that evidence really means, *design* your workplace to meet these needs, *make* it real, then *test* it. Continue the process, again and again, going back to the relevant stage in the process depending on what you discover.

Make it simpler

The more complicated you make your workplace in terms of operation, usability or any other factor, the more complicated it becomes to maintain it and make sure it works properly. In a complex machine, the failure of the smallest part can bring the whole mechanism grinding to a halt, yet the problem can be hard to identify. The simpler the system, the simpler it is to fix.

Why should anything be more complicated than it needs to be, anyway – what purpose could that possibly serve?

People-first organizations function best when they provide just enough structure to thrive, so the same can be said for the human workplaces these platforms manifest. Provide just enough structure to thrive – there is no further reasoning required.

Get the basics right

As with anything in life, if you get the basics right, everything else comes together. There are plenty of old adages around great buildings being built on strong foundations, but it's true. To really build amazing workplaces, we don't need complexity, we need simplicity and function. Workplaces, after all, are the physical element of a platform that's only purpose is to enable a business' people to thrive.

In his experience developing Sky's campus, Neil Usher developed the idea of the *elemental workplace* – a simple proposition whereby a workplace should satisfy a set of basic criteria to provide a platform for its people. Regardless of budget, location, industry, country or culture, these criteria establish the basis for a people-first workplace. Depending on budget, this basic scheme can then be enhanced with features and aesthetics.

Simplifying even further, Neil asserts:

> I usually tell people to fix three things in this order and the rest will follow –
> technology, toilets, coffee.

That might be taking it a little to the extreme, but the point is clear. Getting the essentials right before adding the bells and whistles is nothing more than logic. Do the things that create the most impact.

A beautiful workplace that doesn't meet the basic needs of people and make it easier for them do what they need to do, will never support great work. It will never be the right place for the right people to do the right things.

But why should this point be emphasized so hard? We return to Neil's experience as a workplace professional over more than 25 years:

> … Our sector is mired in the over-complication of the proposition that everyone should enjoy an excellent workplace. We create too many reasons for inaction, rather than considering the potential power of a minimal investment to obtain the maximum benefit from the lowest financial commitment.

Everything else is pointless if you don't get the basics right.

Workstyles and settings

There is an almost infinite combination of possibilities when it comes to the workstyles and work settings your organization offers its people. There's a spectrum between restricted and unleashed approaches, where the parameters that your organization operates in, or the unnecessary complexity it applies, affect both style and setting.

Your workstyle is the way you work. Are your people fixed to a specific location, do they have a level of agility to move around within a particular space, or do they have complete flexibility of movement? Taking it a step further, this links with how you manage the work your people do – is it a question of presence during specific hours, or are they free to work providing they undertake certain actions, achieve certain things or contribute to an agreed level?

Your organization's workstyles provide the evidence that informs the design of the work settings. It's entirely possible and in fact common for different teams to work in slightly different ways, because the parameters around their work are different and each of these requires a different combination of work settings. Quiet space to concentrate, collaborative space to create, meeting space, privacy, social space, all of these requirements are outlined by the collection of data that informs the design process and they need to be provided if your people are to work at their best. Given that the organization's purpose is to enable people to thrive, there's absolutely no excuse not to attend to these needs!

To start to consider your workstyles and settings, work through these basic indicators for every team, based on where you are now and where you could be if your organization was working to freedom within parameters, unleashing its people as humans and enabling them to be their best (see Figure 4.2).

Figure 4.2 Workplace spectrum

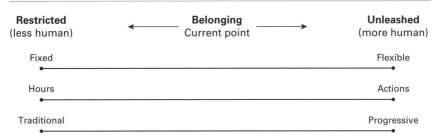

Enabling workstyles through the right settings is an essential part of your success. It informs your strategy and defines what your physical workplace is – whether a single location that people come to every day, a clubhouse they choose to come to for specific purposes, a stadium where they make the most intense connections, or a box where they are controlled and repressed.

For humans to be their best, we need to enable them to be just that. Being human and achieving our best work is about more than just working. Personal wellbeing, social connection, work–life integration and more are all part of the mix, because they're all part of helping people to thrive while they do their best work. These things need to form part of the workplace we provide our people with.

CASE STUDY

Sea Containers: a new kind of workplace

Opened in 2016, Sea Containers created a new landmark headquarters for Ogilvy Group UK, MEC and GTB on London's South Bank. Relocating their businesses from multiple sites across London, 10 semi-autonomous operating companies converged into this one location, creating opportunities for flexibility, collaboration, working and socializing.

The result was a state of the art modern workplace, delivering a range of benefits to all who work there:

- Forty per cent of the building is given over to shared space to support collaboration.
- Shared space receives river views, opening the views to everyone.
- Flexible spaces ensure the availability of the right workspace for any task.
- Hospitality, catering and social spaces rival any in the local area.

- Events are held throughout the building, to help create connections and interactions.
- Art installations create inspiration and stimulus.
- Each brand has its own identified space, while being part of the new collective identity.

Created by BDG architecture + design with Matheson Whiteley, Sea Containers is seen as a new benchmark in workplace design. Taking the best modern workplace thinking and applying it to the building and its inhabitants sympathetically, allowed the creation of a space that enables people to thrive both in their work and personal lives.

Put the slide to bed

Be warned! What works for one workplace does not automatically work for others. Because every organization is a unique collection of individuals congregating around a unique vision, what they need to achieve that vision is unique too.

Your workplace must be designed for *your* people, helping them to thrive and take the actions they need to achieve their best. It's not an investment in space – although real estate professionals would disagree! – it's an investment in people.

There are certain workplaces that, over the years, have received a disproportionate amount of coverage for specific features. Just as table soccer and ping pong tables don't create a culture – but in the right organization can unlock social connection, creative thinking or relaxation – physical features can be a blocker unless they feature in the right places, for the right reasons.

The office slide is a great case in point. Everyone knows about Google's slide and over the years their workplace has received a great deal of press coverage. When BDG architecture + design surveys workers as part of a workplace strategy exercise, one of the questions asked of participants is if they have seen any other space (work or otherwise) that they think the workplace design should take into account. The single most common answer is Google.

Not because they can see how Google's workplace unleashes its people, but because it has a slide and has been heralded by the media as a cool place to work. It's not my place to pass judgement over the effectiveness of Google's approach to workplace, but it provides a great case in point. What works for Google probably won't work for you. Google is Google, with its own vision, behaviours and people. Your organization is equally unique. Unless installing a slide comes with a real benefit, has another authentic reason to be there, or wider issues in business are addressed, it's a gimmick. The same could be said for any feature.

Great workplaces are designed to enable people. That's all they need to do. Anything within them should be added for that reason alone. If a feature can be justified, great. If it can't, don't do it!

If there's a reason to put the slide in, go for it. A reason could be anything that creates positive impact on enabling people. Increased productivity or creativity through allowing play, stimulation of new thinking through alternative perspectives. If there's no reason, put it to bed. Gimmicks don't unleash people.

Waving goodbye to desks?

How we work is undeniably evolving. Every facet of our day to day shifts and changes, regardless of what it is we do for a living. Lorry drivers and factory workers are facing threats from automation (more on that later) and while their work is at present tied to the cabs and lines, these places themselves are also evolving.

Looking at the impact of Sat Nav, or the rise of computing in aiding manufacturing processes, both highlight technology's influence in changing the physical workplace. Offices are experiencing a similar change – and it's an iconic one.

Laptops and tablets, handheld tech and touch screens mean that the office worker no longer needs a traditional base location for a heavy computer or typewriter, with mobile phones disconnecting communication from the desk too. There is less need than ever for an office worker to be tied to a desk or contained in a cubicle and, in an age where collaboration is fuelling progress, all workers need to be unleashed.

Our needs at work are changing – what it takes to enable us to do our best work and even the definition of great work are evolving as quickly as the world around us. Yes, workers will always need the quiet space to concentrate, the changing room or the sluice, but beyond those basic parameters, freedom is now much more … free.

Desks as we know them – pieces of territory, our own little patch of an organization, are becoming outmoded and while surfaces are still required, in a community, it's all about collective contribution, not protected personal space.

Stop giving open plan a hard time

Many of us still seem to be stuck between old thinking and new thinking when it comes to workplace design. We make the mistake of trying to see new ideas through the lens of what's gone before. Open plan is a great case in point.

The real meaning of *open plan* is a space without walls. There are ways to break up spaces and provide a multitude of settings without walls, so open plan is actually a great basis for creating a workplace with light, variety, excitement and identity. It doesn't have to mean a cavernous wide open space full of desks. Great open plan isn't consistent with traditional work styles, but it does support the creation of amazing workplaces that offer every setting an organization's people need – not just to work, but to thrive.

In the age of openness and collaboration, physical walls (just as organizational boundaries) should only be present when there is a reason for them to be so. Legitimate reasons to be there could include privacy, confidentiality, separation as required by the client or health and safety. If there is no reason, walls can unnecessarily reinforce hierarchy, restrict collaboration and breed distrust.

CASE STUDY

Interview: David Atlas

David Atlas is a highly experienced workplace architect, who has worked around the world understanding the link between the physical working environment, the people that work in it and the work they do. He is currently European workplace design director at Nike. Through his career, David has seen the evolution of workplace definition and design, witnessing shifting perspectives on what constitutes an amazing workplace. He shared his views with me.

Looking back at how *workplace* as a concept developed, we see in the pre-WiFi era health problems arising from sedentary work and the stationary nature of the working environment setup. Repetitive strain injury and other physical conditions became more prevalent.

Furniture manufacturers started to focus on the desk and the chair to solve these problems. With the scaling down of desktop computers, hard drives, lighter laptop docking stations and lightweight monitors, the sit/stand desk coupled with advanced flexible seating, we were led to believe that the problems were solved. You could now spend eight hours at a desk, because all the right ergonomics were in place to allow this.

The working world continued to evolve and soon came the realization that a single place of work was not only leading to boring work environments, but also that as technology enabled us to move to more collaborative and flexible types of work, this was not being supported either. At the same time research started to prove that sitting in a single place for most of a day is unhealthy.

Today, the combination of employees moving around the offices to workspaces that suit the task is almost universally recognized as the way forward.

This is driven by three key benefits:

- the creation of settings which suit the different tasks and moods we have;
- the creation of a more interesting, inspiring environment;
- health and wellbeing reasons.

Ignore the phase of gimmicks with slides and ski cabins in the workplace. It was driven by talent attraction, rather than supporting more effective work and today this has largely disappeared. The current move to provide the right spaces offers a more authentic experience.

In a discussion with a former client, he expressed how he wanted the journey of his employees to be once they entered the building. However they arrived at the workplace, they would need to pass through a central social space. From here, you could journey on into the building and find a workspace, or stay for coffee or breakfast in the social space first.

The idea was that it would encourage interaction between colleagues from the very start of the day. It also served as a connected reminder of what the business did, its mission and values, which were expressed in different ways in the social space.

The workplace needs to be an experience for employees. They need to feel connected to the organization, the brand and each other.

To create that experience, an organization needs to be clear on its values, where it wants to go and how it wants the employees to perceive it. Only then can you start to define how the physical space should be.

The workplace experience always needs to be authentic. Employees will see through attempts to create an environment, or an experience which does not genuinely reflect the organization.

Workplace as a service

The final word on the physical workplace in this discussion is that, just like any other aspect of creating a people-first organization, it's an enabler. How your organization's workplace manifests is as individual as the organization itself. Whether a single place, a series of inter-connected or independent locations, a combination of physical spaces and technology that enables remote and home working, the workplace is a system.

Look on your workplace as an app within the organizational platform – an interface and experience that enables your people to do their best work. To really be our best, we need to be enabled not as robots, but as humans – able to be ourselves and contribute in our own way.

The workplace is a subscription service. Your people are the subscribers and it offers them a range of features from which to pick and choose, in order to create the experience that fits their needs and allows them to contribute in their own way. Forget introverts, extroverts, personality types, lifestyles and other complicating factors – if the right options are unleashed, they will provide self-service opportunity for everyone, enabling them to create the optimum conditions for their own best work.

Unlocking traditional benefits too

If you still can't get past the traditional business drivers of cost-saving and short-term investment before unleashing people, then there's good news for you. By using *freedom within parameters* to unleash your people and provide just enough structure to survive, you're able to create clubhouse workplaces.

In these places, flexible working is enabled as far as possible within the parameters, so rather than needing a single workspace, workstation or desk for everyone in the organization, you need to provide the right amount of working spaces to enable them all to work effectively. An unoccupied desk in an office is a wasted space and many organizations find that when they gather their data, up to 56 per cent of desks are unused at any given time.

By collecting the right data and interpreting it effectively in design, it's likely that growth can be supported within the same amount of floorspace you already have, or that you need less space. If this is the case and you can still deliver an amazing workplace that unleashes your people to be their best, whichever way you look at it, there's no argument!

Ten key ideas on place

1 Workplace is the manifestation of the touchpoint between people and organization.

2 It can be physical or virtual.

3 Physical place offers the community a focal point to congregate.

4 Different locations can interpret the same connections in their own way.

5 Workplaces exist only to enable people to do their best work.

6 They should be designed for people through an understanding of what they need to thrive.

7 Basic services should come before gimmicky features.

8 Place offers opportunities to foster collaboration, connection and interaction.

9 Great workplaces also unlock traditional business benefits.

10 Technology is driving constant change in the way we work – our workplaces need to evolve just as fast to keep up.

As the location for connection between people and organization, place has a uniquely powerful opportunity to reinforce that relationship and enable people to do their best work. Understanding what that great work looks like and the actions people need to be empowered to take is the next step in building a human workplace.

Task 5: places for people

This is a quick exploration and assessment tool for your current workplace. Take a look around and follow these questions to create a mood board. You can do it on a blank piece of paper, or download a canvas from the website and the option is yours to make it visual, written, or a combination of the two – it's yours to use and interpret!

- *Who works here?* Describe the people who use this workplace.

- *What do they do?* Outline all the different types of work that take place here.

- *Top three benefits.* Ways your workplace enables great work.

- *Top three frustrations*. Ways your workplace blocks great work.
- *Top three needs*. Simple things that could make the workplace better.
- *Favourite locations*. The best spaces in this workplace.
- *Inspiration*. Where you would work, if you could have any environment.

References

Oswald, J, Proto, E, Sgroi, D (2014) *Happiness and Productivity*, Warwick University.

Usher, N (2012) 'By default, by design – the case against', 5 March. Available from: http://workessence.com/the-case-against-workplace-design/ [Accessed 28 April 2017].

Turning it into action   05

Once you have the right people and the right environments, you have the basis for an amazing, human workplace. It's the platform for your community to do the right things and take the right actions in pursuit of your common quest. Actually unleashing them to take those actions is an art form in its own right.

Traditional management thinking is hung up on complexity, forcing people to work, repeating specific tasks over the course of a number of hours each day. A people-first workplace takes an *untethered view of work*. It's a view through the lens of contribution and freedom within parameters. It's also a view that measures people on what they contribute, not the fact that they're there.

This chapter explores:

- how to enable great work;
- empowering each member of your community to act in its interest;
- tools for creativity;
- an everyday approach for real innovation.

Unleashing work

When you're immersed in complexity, it's difficult to see what's really happening. All you see is the process. When you're providing the minimum viable platform for your people to thrive, in the spirit of design thinking, you can encourage experimentation, individuality, ideas, testing and even failure. It's all part of the journey to great performance.

Management is a mindset, not a method. You can be a manager and still allow your people to thrive, it all depends on the perspective you take. You may allow them to thrive as individuals and trust them to do the right thing; or you may force them to follow a one-size-fits-all process regardless of its suitability for each individual.

Regardless of whether you structure your community in a traditional, hierarchical form or not, if your organization acts as a community, it recognizes that ideas (and the ability to make the best ones real) are key. From that starting point, work can be unleashed to happen in the best possible way – as a reflection of the individual worker, within the parameters set by the community. That's how work becomes unleashed. Performance and developing the ability to be their best becomes the responsibility of each worker, as an adult.

Because the business knows it's providing its people with the right platform to thrive and understands that, as individuals, the exact combination of services and opportunities that each worker needs is unique, it can offer the right level of provision for those people to self-service their best work. That provision is choice, which could cover any area of work, depending how the organization sets itself up. This could include options around technology, communication, workplace, workspace, activity, hours – anything that can enable an individual to work in the best possible way for them.

Here's the key difference:

- the challenge for traditional organizations is how to force people to do their best work;
- the challenge for a human organization is how to enable people to do their best work.

The more you base your platform on control, the less opportunity your people have to innovate, which comes from allowing them the freedom to act. If progressive agility, driven by innovation through design thinking is where the opportunity of future success lies, then it figures that unleashing your people is the way to go.

As with anything, it's a spectrum. How far you decide to go in either direction is down to the way you want to build your platform, based on what your mission is, who the right people are, the behaviours you want to encourage from them and what actions you really want them to take. Take a look at Figure 5.1. Where does your organization sit and where would you like it to?

Think of it as a film, with the members of your community as the assembled members of a cast. At the nucleus there is the director and leading actors, then the supporting cast and crew, then the extras who are involved, but less intensely, then the audience. With the right direction, all know what they need to do to make the scene a success and are able to interpret those directions into their own performance.

Figure 5.1 A scale of freedom and control

| **Control** | **Freedom** |
| (less human) | (more human) |

Some of them need more directing than others, but some are able to improvise completely. Providing the right level of direction to your people is far more important than controlling every minute of their experience at work. Making support and guidance available to those who want and need it is part of providing a platform, but forcing rules on everyone as standard is destructive.

Give your people freedom to act. What's the worst that can happen? They won't always get it right; neither should you want them to. A necessary and essential part of being human is that we make mistakes and learn from them. If you don't allow people to learn through trial and error, they will never develop and remain stagnant. As a result, your organization will stay still, too – or even regress if they are so miserable at their containment that they leave!

The organization needs to provide just the right amount of direction, offer additional support and guidance on a self-service basis and leave the rest open to interpretation. If people are clear on the behaviours they need to exhibit as members of the community, are provided with the right platform (structure, tools and environment) to take them, they have all the parameters they need for great performance.

The job of the organization is to unleash its people to do their best work. As they are all individuals, the route to their best work is their own choice. Treating your people as adults, providing the right platform and services to be great, then giving them the responsibility to get out there and do it, is effective. Your responsibility is the right platform, their responsibility is to use that platform.

If you don't trust your people to take the right actions, then they either aren't the right people, or your platform is ineffective. Don't get hung up on process, or procedure; get hung up on creating the right conditions for (all of) your people to thrive.

Unleash work!

What great means

To really unleash your people and allow them to do great work, they need to understand what *great* actually means. It's part of the parameter that helps drive the right actions and keeps contribution relevant.

Great work is undoubtedly more than a list of tasks to be completed during pre-defined hours, but the organization and people all need to be clear on what that is from the start. Without an understanding of great work, it's impossible to recruit the right people, as there's no understanding of what they are actually expected to do. Equally, it's impossible to build a platform that enables the right people to be great, if that remains undefined.

It's also likely that 'great' in the workplace is more than just work. Traditionally it's been measured as the sum of hours + output, but that's no longer the case. When there's more to strive for through a personal connection with the belief, there's more to contribute than purely task-based yield. This wider immersion in pursuit of a mission happens because we can, because we want to and because we need to.

In most circumstances, great is a combination of expectations, as defined by the individual organization:

- behaviour: the way an individual or group acts;
- contribution: the sum of the actions an individual takes;
- direct tasks: the things required to do an individual's main role;
- indirect tasks: secondary tasks that go beyond the requirements of the main role.

Because your organization is a community, it needs a combination of all of these things to function. I remember the old man who used to put cones out in a church car park next door to my friend's house, to keep the spaces clear for congregation use and stop people like me parking there for social calls. He frustrated us badly and we could never understand why he was so meticulous in his actions, despite not being paid.

That man believed in his community and found this way to contribute, taking responsibility for the actions that he took in pursuit of the community's aims. Maybe this was insignificant in the bigger picture, but it was his way and he owned it. A challenge for all of our organizations is how to empower and inspire our people to behave in a similar way – taking responsibility for a contribution that goes beyond basic participation in the community. That's exactly why a people-focused organization builds itself as a platform. It's also why defining what great actually means is essential.

CASE STUDY

Lee Mallon, founder of Rarely Impossible has spent a great deal of time understanding what great *actually means for his business. These are his reflections:*

Great work is exceeding expectation, you don't wake up in the morning and think *I am going to do great work today*, you fall upon moments in your day where you feel an emotional state of greatness in what you create, those you collaborate with and those you help. In these moments, you surpass your own expectations and that is great work.

Great work tends to be confused with high performance. It is true that great work can result in high performance, but rarely does high performance produce great work. An organization's legacy is not defined by their performance, accolades or profits but for the collective *human* moments that they create – the welcoming smile; a supportive colleague; the customer call that starts at 4.59 pm.

At Rarely Impossible, the definition of great is making life that little bit easier for someone else.

People can only take great action when they understand what great action looks and feels like.

Taking responsibility

Just like the car park man, unleashed people with a clear understanding of what great is need to take responsibility for their contributions.

Responsibility is more ambiguous, because it leaves freedom to act. But you actually *have* to act. If the organization is providing a platform, with all the services you need to be your best, the responsibility for your contribution rests with you – whatever your position in the organization. Those are the parameters. The benefits of being part of this community (whatever they may be) depend on you operating within the parameters of the community by:

- contributing towards the common mission in a pre-agreed way;
- acting in a way that exhibits the agreed behaviours of the community;
- playing an active part in the community.

If an individual wants to remain in the community, this is what they need to do. An investment in supporting their development within the community is required to ensure they have the greatest possible opportunity to thrive. As part of the platform UX, this is the responsibility of the organization. The responsibility of the individual is to make that contribution. As with any community, if you don't adhere to the guidelines or parameters, after fair warning and guidance on how to participate effectively, you will no longer be able to stay as a member.

It may sound harsh, but this is essential for these reasons:

- People who fail to participate and contribute to the community, despite being given every opportunity and guidance to do so, are clearly the wrong people. A great organization starts with the right people.

- Where the platform is right, it is up to the individual to use those services to maximize their contribution. If they are unable to do so – they are the wrong person for that community.

For too long the relationship between organizations and their people has been one of a strict parent and child. You have a right to stay in your family – no matter what you do, ties can never be severed. Human organizations are communities, where adults treat adults like adults. If you have the right platform to thrive and are unable to do so, it's because you are not the right person for the community. Everyone is better to part company at that point. The platform is the responsibility of the organization. Using it effectively is the responsibility of the individual.

Conflicting responsibilities

When we treat people as people, we also need to accept that they *are* people. A human organization is not an altar that comes before all other things, because it recognizes that to contribute effectively, its people must be allowed to be individuals and to do that requires acceptance of the good and the bad.

Because the organization is not an altar at which to be worshipped, it realizes that its people may have other priorities and conflicting purposes in their lives. We discussed earlier how a worker may believe in the organization's purpose, but that their own primary purpose may be to provide for their family. *A human workplace accepts that this is the case.*

School plays, doctors' appointments, sick children, supporting their partner. All of these things are more important than work and rightly so. As an individual, I can contribute better in my work if I focus on it 100 per cent, so I need to deal with other external factors to be able to do that. As long as I'm making my full contribution to the community, then everyone wins.

That's why freedom within parameters is essential – it allows as much flexibility as possible to enable and ensure the maximum contribution at work and outside. As long as the contribution is at the required level, there is no problem.

There's a fine line between responsibility and distraction, though. If personal responsibilities take precedence over work to the point where an individual is consistently unable to contribute, the first question is whether the organizational platform is working effectively to support them and giving them sufficient chance to make the right contribution:

- If the answer is *no*, it's the organization's responsibility to ensure it provides the right platform.
- If the answer to is *yes*, then it's the individual's responsibility to either contribute, or accept that they are not the right person for that community.

Either way, it's an adult relationship, because to function effectively a level of non-dictatorial openness needs to be maintained. Communication must be honest, two-way and consistent. An annual appraisal that highlights how an individual failed to contribute because they were always on the school run doesn't help a person to make their best contribution and do their best work, or the organization to make sure it has the right people, in the right places, doing the right things at all times.

A final note on this. It does challenge traditional contracts of employment and lean towards activity over hours of work, contribution over just pitching up. We've already seen statistics on the effects on productivity of workplace distraction and other factors like stress and lack of sleep. By offering the flexibility to work in a way that allows the individual to be their best, many of these negative impacts can be reduced, while positive impacts around wellness and general happiness can be increased.

Openness

This openness between people and business, with management as the conduit, sounds the death knell for formal periodic feedback. It's OK, because that should be wired into the fabric of a human workplace anyway.

If the organization is structured to enable information to flow freely and instantly in all directions, while the UI and UX combine to make people comfortable with doing so, then a level of honesty and openness will occur naturally.

Actions speak louder than words

There's a reason for this saying. In workplace terms, it's applicable to make sure we get things done. Businesses exist to function and unless the organizational platform is built to encourage action, progress towards the business goal will never be made.

Getting out of the way and reducing complexity and unnecessary distraction as far as possible is the responsibility of the organization. By clearing a path to action, the community is encouraged to act, rather than to hide behind process. By providing the right platform, responsibility for acting is passed to the user (worker) and more will get done. It's the only way to truly unleash people work.

Where tradition has been based on micromanagement and control, being able to get out of the way of work is one of the most difficult and daunting things an organization or any size, scale and at any level can do. It requires trust and the knowledge that when you turn your back, the action will continue. We all know that in most cases once the boss is out of the way, everyone relaxes and that's where the old ways were broken.

In a human workplace, by taking accountability for our own work we avoid reliance on bosses to force us to do it. The organization itself is structured to allow that to happen. If we're not contributing, we're not playing our part in the community; therefore we run the risk of not being part of it. If we want to do nothing for a whole week, then work for 48 hours at the weekend, as responsible workers that's our prerogative. As long as the contribution falls within the parameters required by the business, why should it be any other way?

Minimum viable effort

Minimum viable effort is the least amount of effort that can be expended to achieve a desired outcome. Whether you're building the organizational platform, or taking the actions you need to take to contribute effectively, there is no reason to make it any harder than it needs to be. In the age of minimum viable everything, minimum viable effort is a perfectly valid approach to work.

In the animal world, a theory called *the energetic definition of fitness* predicts that animals that expend less energy will have more energy for survival and reproduction (Walker, 2009). The same stands for organizations and the people that work in them. The less energy you spend on unnecessary things, the more you have available for getting stuff done.

Minimum viable effort is nothing more than simplification. There is absolutely no valid reason to make things any more complicated than they need to be. The more complicated something is, the harder it becomes to achieve. A lack of complexity does not mean a lack of hard work, it just means clarity over what the right work is. The removal of unnecessary hoops to jump through to achieve your contribution to the organization gives workers two things – more time to contribute and more time to enjoy.

The biggest culprit for expending unnecessary energy in the workplace and over-complicating things that just don't need to be anything other than simple, is meetings. Formal meetings are a series of words, which create barriers to action. Conversations, on the other hand, drive productivity.

Not so nice to meet you

Meetings. Everybody seems to hate them, yet everybody seems to have them. In a presenteeism-driven workplace, having the most meetings has become a badge of importance. Unfortunately, it's no measure of achievement. Scheduling rounded hours in calendars can fill a day with formal forums for conversations that may really need to take minutes. Meetings also get in the way of doing actual work.

I remember my first management position. Each week there was a meeting of the managers within the unit, ironically called the 'Action Group'. There was much fanfare around booking a room – usually 10 minutes' walk from where our offices were all clustered together around the same corridor, providing catering and making sure that everyone attended. The conversations were minuted and formally distributed for review prior to the meeting.

Once congregated and the extended niceties, coffee pouring and biscuit passing were out of the way, the meeting proceeded like this:

- review and approval of the previous meeting's minutes, usually involving some minor amendments for the record that really would have no bearing on anything;
- review of previous action points, dealing with always-unfinished items to this meeting's agenda;
- item-by-item conversation on this meeting's agenda and setting of actions, to be reviewed in the next meeting;
- individual progress updates where people spoke for far too long in an attempt to prove how busy they had been since the last meeting;
- any other business – where unnecessary conversation reached a whole new level.

Even though the reasons for the meeting may have been valid, by spending time discussing what we would, could and should do, we were wasting time and energy on theory, while actually preventing ourselves from doing it. When things get done, the results speak for themselves. They don't need a specific forum to be highlighted, because if the organizational platform is right, recognition should happen naturally.

There are books written on ways to have better meetings and many strategies. For starters, try these things:

- only hold a formal meeting where strictly necessary;
- only use a formal meeting room where strictly necessary;
- diarize only a small, clearly specific block of time, say 17 minutes;
- stick to that time;
- only discuss what needs to be discussed;
- move on as quickly as possible.

Actions always speak louder than words. When you take actions, you move towards your goals. You don't get anywhere by standing still!

Stop and ask why

The only way to avoid over-complication and expending anything other than the minimum viable energy in getting things done is to *question everything*. In a human workplace, the fundamental question that should be asked around everything is *why*?

There has to be a reason for everything you do and that reason has to be the right one. Reason creates purpose and without purpose, there is no point. Doing things for the right reasons is central to the human organizational platform and the responsibility for making sure that is the case belongs to everyone.

An organization that doesn't allow itself (and the individuals within it) to be constantly analysed is a platform ready to fail. Think of it like a piece of software – when something crashes, or you find a bug, you report it. The users of the system (your workers) need to be given the channels to report their findings as they test your system.

Whether you open those channels or not, your users will find bugs. It's far better that you know about them, than force the conversation and reporting underground to become negativity.

Question everything, at all times. It's the only way to find an alternative perspective.

Living and breathing it

If every member of the community is empowered with direct contribution to its evolution and success, they are able to take ownership of it. Ownership doesn't need to be about shares, or finances, it can be as simple as feeling like your voice matters – like you are a real part of the community.

Community is based on connection. The different connections between the individuals, teams, collaborators and sub-communities at all levels within the community are what enables the business to progress and drive forward towards its goal. Where these connections work in a way that unleashes both action and information, they create impact benefits that allow the business to progress through constant iteration and innovation.

These include:

- increased perspectives, fuelling ideas;
- wider, constant insights;
- connection between business and people (consumer and internal);
- the ability to act faster;
- designs thinking as standard.

Human workplaces live and breathe action, because they get out of the way enough to let it happen. In doing so, they divert focus onto contributing towards the common mission, by unleashing everyone to do their best work and own it. The stronger the connection between people and business, fostered by the organization, the more effective the contribution. Human organizations unleash people, to be living, breathing people in the workplace. They are individuals and that brings real benefit.

The right actions, on your own terms

If you need someone to take the right actions, why would you do anything other than get out of the way and let them take them? As long as the outcome is the right one, or the action is in the interests of the business, there is absolutely no good reason to intervene, or dictate the method of getting there. *Parameters are necessary, rules are autocratic.*

Trial and error are part of design thinking, which makes failure not only allowable, but positively encouraged in a human workplace. Without empowering people to learn through trying things, it's impossible to progress and experimentation always has a risk of failure.

Not only is failure a good learning mechanism and driver of development, allowing people to act on their own terms recognizes that each of them is an individual. As an individual, the actual actions I might take, when I take them, my chosen method and other aspects of my approach, are unique to me. A colleague might take a completely different approach to reach the same level of contribution, but that should be their prerogative.

If the goal is to have people contributing and participating, allowing them to be stimulated by taking those actions in their own way, on their own terms, encourages them to perform better. Prescribing a set of specific actions that must be taken in a certain way, in a certain place, at a certain time (except where dictated by the parameters you're operating within), is counter-productive.

People are more productive when they are motivated and more motivated when they have freedom and choice. Giving it to them is the least you can do.

Contribution, productivity and output

In most workplaces, productivity is measured by output. At an individual level, this is linked to the completion of specific tasks within specific timescales. In a linear world, that's fine, because things can be measured in a linear way. Selling more, producing more, growing more, it's all measurable.

Contribution and the space to do so are completely different things. They aren't directly quantifiable, but they give rise to the benefits of people participating. By allowing ideas, information and interactions to flow, they create a dynamic, adaptive community, that can change before it becomes obsolete.

It's an ever-active network, where the right information is on hand at any given time to drive the next stage of progress. Impact can be measured, just as output can and where a clear direction is combined with an enabling platform, success – however that is defined – can be achieved.

Short-term linear growth approaches may work initially, but they are never sustainable. Sustainability comes from evolution, which itself comes from innovation via design thinking and the pairing of insight with creativity and action.

An attendance record is no more a measure of performance than an employer's reference is a genuine marque of quality. Human workplaces thrive on impact through contribution, and this requires a different kind of measurement. Whether through peer-to-peer ratings, customer (community) feedback, recognition mechanisms, activity, or any combination of measures (potentially including some traditional ones), defining and measuring contribution is an essential part of building the organizational platform. It provides a clarity of expectation around the activity expected of each member of the community.

Each organization is individual, driven by a unique shared mission and populated by a unique set of people. What great looks like and how to measure it needs to be defined by each organization. There is no one-size-fits-all method.

Ebb and flow

A major flaw with linear measures is that they expect a consistent level of performance. Standard working hours, as defined by contracts of employment, assume that every individual within an organization is able to work at their optimum level at pre-allotted hours.

Those of us who have ever been tired, distracted, on a roll or full of ideas, know that's just not the case. We've already seen how sleep deprivation costs businesses billions each year in lost productivity and when correlating that against the stress statistics we also saw, an idea of the connection between wellness and productivity emerges. If people are too tired, distracted or otherwise unable to work effectively at any given point in time, why make them? What we need is their best work, not their maximum time. Hours are a parameter that should be removed unless they are completely necessary. Freedom within parameters means we should only apply the very minimum of structure, in order to unleash our people to work.

As humans, our moods, energy, concentration levels and focus ebb and flow. It's why building wellness into the working environment is essential and also why allowing the work itself to be done as flexibly as possible is prudent. If I'm hit by a wave of inspiration at 10 pm on Sunday, waiting to do anything about it until 9.30 am on Monday is a missed opportunity for everyone.

Work needs to allow for the rhythms of life, which are different for each of us. As long as the worker is able to make the right contribution, what else matters? Anything other than the minimum of structure is unnecessary complication – the addition of a moving part that could go wrong. This is all part of the ebb and flow of performance. If you want an individual to be able to do their best work (which every organization does), provide the conditions that allow it to happen. Give them the opportunity to self-service what they need, to fit their work around their ebb and flow.

Creative work

Creativity is the creation of an alternative perspective. As an idea and a word, it is often misunderstood in the workplace, seen as the preserve of industries recognized under a definition of 'creative'. How many of us truly believe that we can be creative in our work? Even the most seemingly mundane tasks are open to creativity, because it's a mindset, not a definition. Rethinking our view on something, creating a new perspective, approaching a task in a different way – it's all creativity, even if the end result isn't a graphic illustration or architectural design.

I recently sat in on a conversation around creativity held by the European Union in Brussels, where a professor asserted that too much focus is being paid to creativity and innovation whereas a complete overhaul of a broken education system is needed. Surprised, my only response was to ask but *how will we achieve that without creativity and innovation?* Such things are the fuel that drives progress!

How will we ever do anything differently if we're unable to access the new perspectives, connections, approaches and ideas that creativity affords us? There's no real argument against it. Humans by nature are creative. Even if we don't know or acknowledge it, as social animals our predisposition is to investigate, explore, consider and question.

My belief is that everyone not only has the opportunity to be creative in their work, but that they have the capability – it just needs to be unlocked and unleashed. Often, that's as simple as allowing it to happen via the organizational platform by connecting people, encouraging collaboration, experimentation and freedom.

Nothing can be lost by promoting creativity in any workplace; as long as the right contributions happen, the business only serves to gain from this approach. Understanding that creativity is a state of mind – not a pre-defined action – and reframing it that way in the workplace is the key to unleashing it. Most organizations outside what is deemed to be the 'creative industries' fail to actively promote creativity as a mindset, because they don't see the value of doing so. Everyone can bring benefit to their workplace through a creative mindset, because as with design thinking, it constantly tests the platform.

Heart and soul

Whether it's work, play, family, whatever, we're able to give our best when we're able to fully express ourselves. If we can pour our heart and soul into something, because we believe in it and we're enabled to contribute fully in our own way, we can give it everything. Humans function best when they have an identity, a cause, something to believe in.

Anything that dilutes or blocks our ability to connect and contribute is a layer of detriment. It strips some of our human potency and potential, preventing it from contributing.

Traditionally, workers have been uniformed and judged. Those who keep their heads down and stay within the confines of dictated behaviour are able to 'get along'. Being different equates with trouble, which is understandable in a way. Our fight or flight mechanism is based around recognized structures. If we don't recognize it, it scares us and we avoid it.

Individuality contributes to alternative perspectives and agile adaptability, through ideas. In the modern world, organizations need to harness these traits to compete now and keep pace into the future. Embracing the individuality and humanity of each member of the community supercharges everything from organizational development to product development, because it encourages the widest possible collection of perspectives.

- The wider the sample, the more effective the identification of trends.
- More perspectives mean more ideas.
- More connections mean more possible collaborations.
- More freedom means quicker response.

All of these things contribute to shaping the performance of the community and the success of the business in driving for its goals.

Accessing individuality

Plugging into the individuality of each person in the community means taking every aspect of them. It means accepting the emotions, contradictions and other variables that make us human. In a human organization that strives for simplicity, the humans themselves are the most complex part! Far from being a negative thing, this can be harnessed positively to enhance the individual and collective contributions to the community, allowing it to function better.

Creativity comes from dark places. Some of the best albums, artworks and literature have come from darkness. It's not all play and bright colours. Sometimes to truly think differently, a level of intensity provided by discomfort or restriction can be just as, if not more, effective at creating new perspectives. It's why human workplaces are so able to foster creativity.

Not only does the free flow of information and connection allow limitless unique combinations, but by encouraging and allowing everyone to be their full, unedited selves, they are able to bring the light and the dark to make a full contribution.

It's not unprofessional to be emotional, hurt, sick, weak, fragile or distracted. It's human.

What if …

- I need to alter my working hours around a non-work pastime?
- My insomnia means I'm too tired in the day, but thinking freely at night?
- I'm suffering from anxiety?
- I just want to be somewhere different today?

Does it make me any less able to contribute, or does it potentially make my contribution more unique?

If we suppress human traits, we will never have access to the full potential contribution of the individual. Without that, the organization can never function at its optimum and the community suffers. There's a difference between demonstrating shared behaviours and being repressed into a stripped-down, nondescript worker.

Any organization that is unable to discern one employee from the other because they all dress the same, act the same, follow the same routines and processes is stripped of the human element of its platform. People cannot be enabled when they're prevented from being people.

What creativity looks like

When people are enabled to be themselves, contribution and creativity are unlocked in the organization. It's an almost natural by-product of unleashed information in a freedom within parameters organization, enabled by the platform.

The most successful creative work comes from allowing people to be people and express themselves in new ways. It all starts with an understanding of what you are trying to achieve and the context you're trying to achieve it in. Creative thinking can be applied to anything, anywhere and although removing the tethers and allowing complete freedom of thought is a key part of it, bringing it back to something that's deliverable in the real world is equally important.

We return to the funnel again. The creative process needs to throw as many ideas and perspectives into the top as it possibly can, before filtering them to find the best ones and develop them in a way that can *actually be made real*.

It's alleged that Thomas Edison once said, 'Idea without action is hallucination.'

There are various viewpoints on whether Edison actually said this, or someone else entirely, but it makes a great point. You can have the best ideas in the world, but unless you do something about them and make them real, they are nothing but a pie in the sky waste of time!

This applies to anything. From developing your organization to launching a new product, creativity is a mindset and to harness it, you need to turn it into action.

Head space is a great starting point. Giving people (physical and mental) room to think differently in their daily work allows creativity to thrive. If a more focused outcome is needed, or a specific question is to be answered, as long as you understand what you are trying to achieve, you can develop the right experience around it. In my own work unlocking creativity in some of the world's most prominent brands from the fast moving consumer goods, pharmaceutical and media industries, these experiences have been as diverse as:

- immersive ideation and development through hands-on making;
- game show-style experiences (including *Masterchef* and *Shark Tank*);
- scientific forums to bring interactivity;
- creating vessels to launch movie characters.

These experiences have contributed to new product development, technology applications, packaging designs, business transformations and more. The what and why of these is unimportant, they are listed to highlight that anything is possible. I often think that my work has succeeded when the aftermath resembles a kids' party! There are no rules in creative work, just the right actions and it all starts with understanding and context. These things create direction and purpose, just as a business' mission drives the organization forward. Creativity looks and feels different, that's all you need to know. Because if doesn't, then you're doing the same as you always do and will continue to get the same (or worse) outcomes.

Fostering creativity

Creativity is the basis for innovation. It's a perfect precursor but it should never be mistaken for innovation in itself. If you start by considering a problem or question creatively, you will have the right starting point for innovating the right answers. *Creativity* is about having the ideas. *Innovation* is about doing something with them.

TOOL 1 Creativity worklist

Here's a step-by-step approach for fostering creativity in your organization, useful and applicable for any purpose. It all starts with the right question. Any exploration needs to have a purpose. If you don't have one, you won't progress.

Before you start the exploration, ask whether you actually know what it is you want to know! Unless you have a goal, however broad, in mind, it will be too aimless. Spend some time defining the question you want to ask, then work through the list below to create the conditions for creatively exploring your question.

1. Environment

Look on creativity as creating idea seeds to be grown into amazing innovations. Like any seeds, ideas need fertile ground.

The right environment for creativity is:

- safe;
- open;
- participatory.

If people are afraid of judgement (from managers, colleagues, peers or anyone else), they will hold back. If people are unable to contribute, they will hold back. If people are excluded, they will hold back.

To create the right environment, you need to go beyond the obvious. People contribute in different ways. Some are comfortable speaking in front of others, some aren't. Your challenge is to create the environment that not only tells people they can contribute, but helps them to do so, by enabling participation.

Within this environment, it's essential to communicate and prove that at this stage, there are no wrong answers. At the very top of our creative funnel, we want the most diverse set of possibilities to explore and filter.

A good creative process means that often the best starting points are as far from the obvious or deliverable as is possible. Create the environment that allows these to emerge.

2. Stimulus

We need to catalyse our brains to think creatively. Creating connections with other perspectives is one way, but providing stimulus in other ways is essential too. How can you inspire people to think differently?

Often we see workshops with pens and post-it notes, but the exploration is held in a dingy conference room with nothing that catalyses. There are three main types of stimulus to employ:

1 *Physical.* What items can you bring into the environment that encourage exploration and connect with the senses? Consider lateral and abstract ideas.

2 *Mental.* What are the questions and provocations you can use to ignite thinking? How can you create scenarios that take thinking in new and interesting directions?

3 *Tools.* What are you giving your people to create and capture these ideas? Remember that people work in different ways, some like to write, some like to draw, some like to build. Giving people a tool they're not used to, or comfortable with, can focus their contribution in new ways.

Restriction can be just as powerful as completely unrestricted thought, so paying attention to the right experience will help to drive the right outcomes. Sound familiar?

3. Potential

The overall experience, combined with the environment (physical or virtual) you create and the stimulus you provide will define your people's ability to contribute. Bringing together the right mix of people is equally important.

The more diverse the population involved, the more diverse the perspectives will be. The connection of these different perspectives is where the magic really happens, so the more of this you allow to happen, the more exciting the outcome.

You're probably thinking of this in a micro-level workshop, but the rule follows for any aspect of an organization, at any scale. The more diverse a population, the more progressive it can be.

A team of engineers solving an engineering problem will perpetuate an engineering point of view. Mix them with other people from other backgrounds and even some wildcard contributors. The limit is your imagination and that limits theirs!

A team of organizational development professionals developing an organization will perpetuate an organizational development perspective. They should only be part of the mix at the ideation stage.

To creatively consider anything, create the right environment, add the right stimulus and bring together the most diverse set of perspectives you can, geographically, professionally and culturally. You'll reap the benefits.

TOOL 2 Positive answers

In tandem with the creativity worklist, I developed an approach that can be used by anyone to creatively explore any question, challenge or issue they may have, and I want to share the basis of it with you here. It's called *positive answers* and is based on a popular technique. By using it, you create new perspectives on problems that allow you to break your thinking beyond the restrictions of the structures your brain works within.

Here's what to do:

- Write down your problem or question.
- Explore it using a creative thinking technique.

I use six staple approaches:

1 *Instinct*. Count down from three, then write the first thing that comes into your head. See what happens when you trust yourself.
2 *Brainstorm*. Purge your brain of every thought and idea on this question for two minutes. See what gems lurk in your unleashed mind.
3 *Meditate*. Take some time out, relax and empty your mind. Come back when you're refreshed.
4 *Walk*. Go for a walk outside, tune into the world and think about your problem. What answers will the great outdoors give you?
5 *Draw it*. Pick up a pencil and doodle a way to solve the problem. Let the visual perspectives emerge.
6 *Super hero*. Take on the personality and powers of a superhero. How would they solve the problem?

Where possible, I'd bring in a seventh:

7 *Build it*. Be less literal and build a perspective using LEGO, straws, matchsticks or anything else you can get your hands on.

Use one or more of these techniques to *create one to three seed solutions* to your questions. They can be as abstract and fanciful as you like at this stage. Write each one on a piece of paper.

Take one of your answers and *swap them* with someone else's answer to a different question. This is your starting point for considering your problem!

It's likely this seed answer will be undeliverable within budget, the laws of physics or reason, but in trying to explore the idea and apply it to your own question, you will have a completely new perspective that breaks all the limits of your own thinking. From there you can work back in.

Positive answers developed into a card deck to take itself one step forward. By equipping everyone in a team, or even an organization with this tool, you can unleash constant exploration that starts from a completely disconnected position, before working back to connect with reality. It's regularly used in workshops to explore everything from leadership challenges to product and service ideation. Featuring question, answer and approach cards, users build up a selection of questions and answers. They can shuffle their own decks to get new perspectives at any time, or swap cards with others to expand that even further.

It's a simple, but powerful tool that creates new perspectives and alternative approaches wherever and whenever they are needed.

Real innovation

When you explore a question creatively, you feed the funnel at the top. These seed answers are plentiful and all have potential, but to turn into action and really grow into something that benefits the business or organization, they need to be cultivated. The first step is filtering the ideas by identifying which seeds are worth developing. There really is only one way to do this – the power of the crowd.

Ask the actual people concerned with the solution, which ideas they think are most ripe for development. Whether that's those participating in a workshop, your internal or external community, a specific team, or another group, the best insight into what these people need rests with the people themselves. Make sure you tap into it!

Develop a shortlist of ideas to take forward to the next stage, depending on your capacity and resources. Once you have your filter and decide which ideas to work on, it's time to take them forward and do the work.

Suggestion: pick a wildcard idea for further exploration sometimes, too. You never know where it might lead!

TOOL 3 Developing ideas

Once you have a seed idea to develop, you can grow it towards real action. Don't jump straight into implementing something; the first step is to explore the seed idea further. At the moment, it's nothing but a speck of information and insight!

First, understand what you're looking at and consider the possibilities:

- *Need.* What problem are you solving?
- *Experiment.* What happens if you look at the problem in alternative ways? This is where a range of perspectives comes in very useful.
- *Brainstorm.* Throw all the thoughts you have around this idea onto a sheet of paper.
- *Anything's possible.* Start with 100 per cent freedom and think about how you would approach this idea if there were no limits. You can add the parameters in the next stage of development.

Once you've spent some time really understanding your idea in these terms, you can use the explorations to start understanding how you could deliver the idea in a way that makes the most positive impact. This is where things get more focused around what's deliverable and how they can be delivered.

Your next mission is to develop the *what, why* and *how*. This is the basis for real action:

- *Name.* Every idea is a miniature brand. You'll need people to buy into it, so start thinking of it in those terms.
- *Audience.* Understanding who this idea is aimed at will help guide you in what its final form looks like and how to deliver it.
- *Description.* This is where you start to put some detail, by outlining what you are delivering.
- *Visualization.* Sketch it out. No matter how simple or detailed your drawing is, creating a visual representation of any answer helps to start bringing it to life.

Next, you can start to think about something really important – action!

TOOL 4 Planning action

From the information you've started mapping out about your idea, you can think about the journey that brings it to life. Work through these areas:

- *Starting point.* What's the very first thing you need to do to achieve progress?
- *Positive action.* Define the single most important action you can take to gain momentum. The one thing that will rocket boost the idea forward.
- *Team.* Who does this idea need to make it happen? Remember that diversity of perspective is important.
- *Partnerships.* Think about any external collaborations that could support the development.

This puts a wrapper of reality around your ideas and gives you the first steps towards a plan. Use them to define:

- *Top three actions.* Once started, think about the most powerful things you can do to chase progress.
- *Dependencies.* What external factors could impact the development of the idea (consider obstacles as well as boosters)?

These explorations form the basis for any exploration in idea development. I use them regularly to form approaches tailored to specific circumstances. They aren't the all-inclusive answer and you might find your specific context has an additional consideration or requirement, but they are a good base to start from.

The canvas is an excellent way to visually represent these questions and access the exploration in a well-mapped way. They are easily shared, support collaboration and can be updated fast. See Figure 5.2 for a universal idea development canvas.

Figure 5.2   Idea development canvas

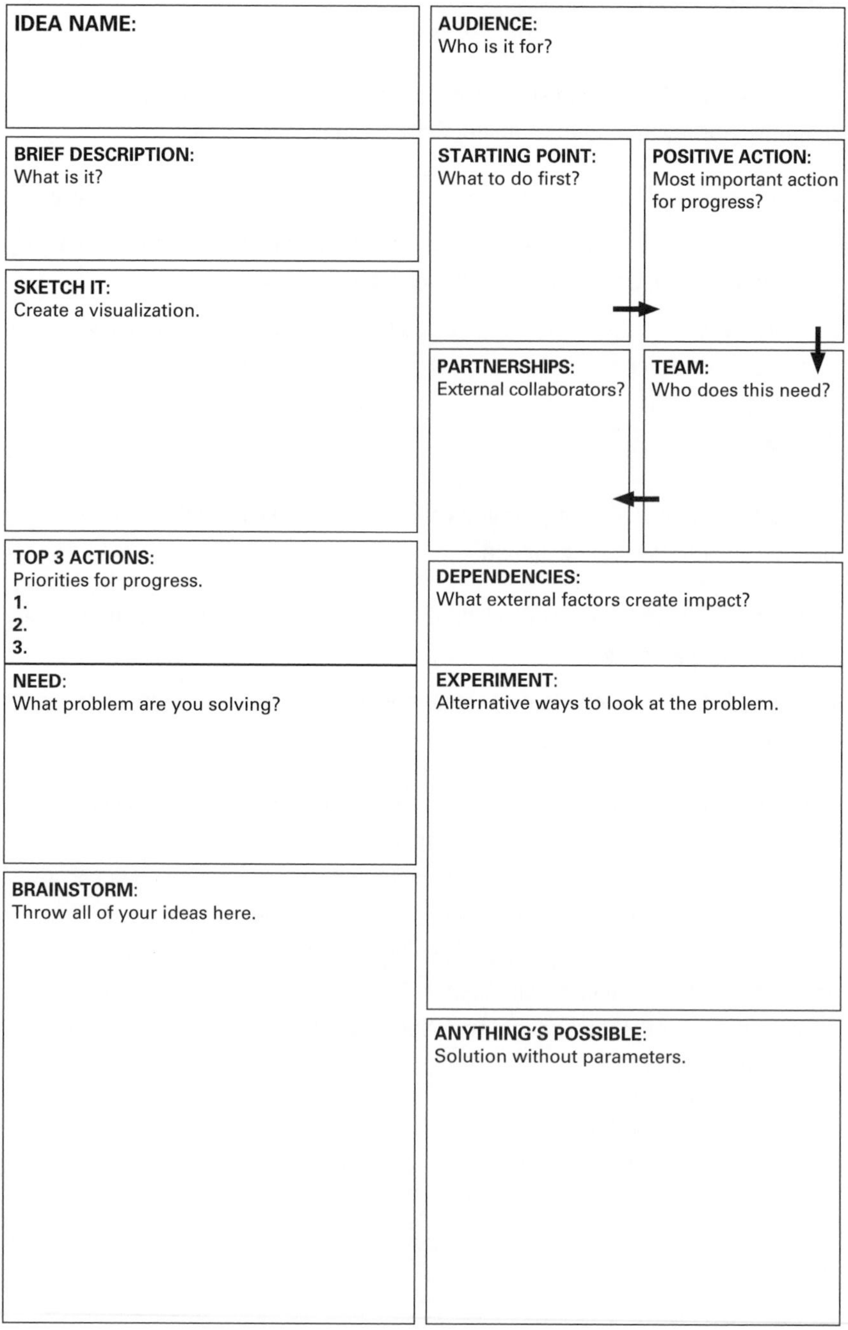

IDEA NAME:	AUDIENCE: Who is it for?	
BRIEF DESCRIPTION: What is it?	**STARTING POINT:** What to do first?	**POSITIVE ACTION:** Most important action for progress?
SKETCH IT: Create a visualization.	**PARTNERSHIPS:** External collaborators?	**TEAM:** Who does this need?
TOP 3 ACTIONS: Priorities for progress. 1. 2. 3.	**DEPENDENCIES:** What external factors create impact?	
NEED: What problem are you solving?	**EXPERIMENT:** Alternative ways to look at the problem.	
BRAINSTORM: Throw all of your ideas here.	**ANYTHING'S POSSIBLE:** Solution without parameters.	

TOOL 5 Taking them somewhere

Any great idea needs someone to take it forward. You already identified your team in the last stage, but now you need an investor to get behind it. An investor can be any or all of these:

- budget holder with the funds to support your idea;
- strategic stakeholder who can approve it;
- target market who will adopt it.

Essentially, every idea needs a sponsor or an advocate. However your organization is structured, ideas need to support if they are to become action. Even if it's something very small, by gaining support you minimize the risk it involves and add just the right amount of common sense checking before you embark on making it real.

Ideas need to be pitched! Although it might sound serious, or laborious, or like an added level of complexity where management approval is required, it's not. This is just a way of testing your idea before you go all-in on it. You don't have to pitch to your direct superior and hopefully, your team will be so diverse and cross-profession that there will be no single superior to pitch to. You just need to find the right person who can sponsor the idea and take it forward.

If you can't find one of those, you have two choices: 1) refine the idea and re-pitch; 2) carry on anyway.

Both approaches have merits. We'll discuss the second later, as positive activism can be powerful and important. The less risky option is always the first and 'risk' is the operative word.

Many of us have seen *Shark Tank* (or *Dragons Den*), the TV show where businesses pitch their ideas to potential investors in a bid to win funding. By pitching your idea, you are convincing a potential sponsor that your idea is worth their investment. One of the key aspects of a human workplace is that everything is done for the right reasons, in the interest of the business. Pitching to a sponsor is a way of ensuring that those reasons are there and making sure you haven't missed anything.

All ideas involve certain types of risk and positive impact, particularly:

- business;
- commercial;
- financial;
- reputation.

Each of these needs to be considered for best- and worse-case scenario, to get a picture of the overall risk and impact the idea is likely to bring. Your idea will fit into one of the areas shown in Figure 5.3.

Figure 5.3   Risk and impact

Any of these risk profiles is potentially investable, but that depends on the appetite for risk you, the sponsor and the organization has, as well as who is willing to take responsibility for it. If you pursue a high risk, high-impact idea without a sponsor, you will either be the saviour of the business, or out of the community. Because, even if you have freedom to fail, it can be argued that the stakes were just too high to go it alone and in doing so you weren't acting in the interests of the community. Everyone in a human workplace wants to make things happen. We just need to do it in the right way that fits the community.

Allowing innovation to happen

Once an idea has its sponsor, it has a level of ownership and accountability from the team and its representative. That drives action. The members of the team can keep each other and the sponsor focused and the vice versa. This is where it becomes a project. Managing the development of the idea into something deliverable will require a list of tasks, people to do them and a timescale to do it. Don't over complicate it – map those things out and get started!

Tweak as you go, but make sure you *keep moving forward*. Following the design thinking route, forward progress may actually mean going back to an earlier step in the process sometimes, but that's a very productive thing to do. This project now takes the idea into a *minimum viable* state and aims to get it out into its audience community to pilot and test in a state of perpetual beta, constantly developing and refining it in perpetuity.

Insight before labs

Just as creativity is often seen as the preserve of the creative industries, innovation is often shoehorned into a box. Innovation labs have seen huge investment in organizations over recent years. While they have undoubtedly had some success, this model is hugely limited.

We've looked at how every idea is the result of a unique piece of inspiration, formed through a potent combination of connection and collaboration. That's the only way to take it forward, too. In a human organization, any project or piece of work needs the right team to do it and they may come from anywhere in the community. That doesn't change lines of reporting or organizations structure, it changes the flow of information and the unleashing of collaboration.

Where an organization invests in a single team to sit inside an innovation lab detached from the day-to-day of the business, it gains focus on innovation per se, but loses connection. Connection unlocks insight and information, which is where the seeds of innovation come from.

Rather than invest in innovation labs, human workplaces invest in:

- connection;
- collaboration;
- cross-pollination;
- allowing the right teams to emerge for any project.

Creating the place and space for that team to thrive in its innovation is essential too. That's a real lab!

CASE STUDY

An innovation perspective: Sanjay Patel

Sanjay is a seasoned cross-functional and cross-category innovator with over 20 years' experience in creative leadership and driving change. Previously with Astra Zeneca and PZ Cussons, Sanjay now works in Global Innovation for The

Coca-Cola Company, discovering irrefutable insights and translating them into business opportunities. We discussed his approach.

Why is it important for businesses to unleash innovation?

Innovation is the lifeblood of progress. Without it we would have not moved on from living in caves. As societies, environments, geopolitical and financial landscapes evolve, an organization needs to be nimble enough to at least swim with the shoal, if not lead it.

How can they do that?

Many people think that it is about a process, but a process is just a tool that needs to be wielded correctly and in my mind that counts for about 10 per cent of the right answer. The remaining 90 per cent is behaviour and environment, it's as simple as that.

Employees need to know that they are trusted to be a bit out there, try something new, make mistakes and be acknowledged (if not rewarded) for trying. Typically, short-term planning and deliverables get in the way of deeper thinking, trying something new or looking out over the two- to three-year horizon to create something revolutionary versus something evolutionary.

Ring-fenced resource (human and financial) is one approach, but a better one is to create a culture of innovation and intrapreneurship that is supported right from the top and driven across every level and function of the business.

What is your approach?

Spike Lee summed it up pretty well in the title of his film *Do the Right Thing*.

I have always used the Michael Porter shared value trifecta for sustainable growth as a North Star for success in everything I do. This calls for environmental prosperity, societal prosperity and a reasonable economic gain for everyone involved in the route to market.

Once you have those insights identified, you need to bring them to life in a very visceral way so that everyone gets it immediately. I typically follow this insight based ideation with a 'sprint' or a 'hack' with the lead ideas at the end of this stage.

I also ensure that the lead routes are presented to a very senior level of the leadership team straight after the session, almost like a *Dragon's Den* or *Shark Tank* with budget on the table for progression. This ensures business focus and impact as well as a bit of carrot or stick for those working on the idea ... all in a fun way of course!

Do you have any tips for companies looking to find and develop their next big idea?

Insight, insight and more insight. I call it the hunt for the irrefutable insight. People get hungry, people get cold, people want to be happy and feel loved, that kind of thing.

If the foundation is weak, the ideas that follow will also typically be quite shallow and not that great. Those involved in the creative process need to work hard on making the question and your proposed answer as easy to understand and endorse as possible. Some people call it the elevator pitch, but that can be fraught with internal jargon in my experience. A brief in a tweet and explaining the answer to a five-year-old is a better methodology. If you can't do either of these, then the work is not complete!

Further thoughts on innovation

Innovation has been a big buzz word for the last 15 years or so with departments being set up and many creative agencies building extremely good livings from not being particularly good. I still attend sessions being run by external partners where the facilitator seems to think that throwing some bean bags on the floor and giving everyone a 'Post-it' note block is all there is to it. No insight, no immersion and very weak facilitation.

A workshop is a living process. As soon as it starts you can almost throw away the detailed game plan as the attendees' behaviour on the day and in that environment will dictate how the session goes. Facilitators often forget the simple human things like people feeling hungry, tired, cold or lost in the process and then fail to adjust what they are doing to counteract this.

Making my workshops an amazing experience for the attendees is my first and foremost concern, because if people are happy they do great work. The biggest compliment I receive is when attendees ask if they can be trained to do what I do, or request another session.

Thinking and acting by design

When work is unleashed, it's able to drive relentlessly forward through people, because the people are driven to take action and given the right tools to do so. Whichever way you look at it, every aspect of work, collaboration, creativity and innovation (traits of human workplaces) tie in with the ideas of design thinking. Figure 5.4 shows how.

It's a fluid, open system of work. The organization doesn't need to be structured in a particular way, it just needs to be enabled so that work is unleashed. When that happens, the community can thrive and the platform that allows them to do that can continue to evolve in a state of perpetual beta, just like the products and services the organizations creates. That's because it is one.

Figure 5.4   How design thinking manifests

DESIGN THINKING	WORK
Understand	Connection (insight)
Think	Collaboration (idea)
Design	Action (development)
Make	Minimum viable
Test	Perpetual beta

Figure 5.5   The simple, better, human question

QUESTION	ACTION
How can it be simpler?	Remove complexity
How can it be better?	Improve outcomes
How can it be more human?	Create a connection

Reaching this point means the organization has managed to look beyond unnecessary complexity and unlock the things that allow it to be as powerful and progressive as it can be. It's shed a layer (or more) of skin and is continually fresh and dynamic, purely because it allows itself to be.

Because of the paradox of people being the most necessarily complicated variables in an organization, we know from experience that if we're not vigilant complexity creeps back in. Part of everyone's role in the community is to make sure that doesn't happen. Some time ago, I discovered three simple questions that help to assess and, when turned into actions, maintain the humanity in any workplace by eliminating the unnecessary aspects of 'business'. These are set out in Figure 5.5.

It's the most powerful management tool I've ever discovered – so powerful I built my company around it – and is something we can all bring to our work every single day.

Ten key ideas on action

1 Human workplaces enable people to do their best work.

2 To do great work, people need to know what great is.

3 A human workplace takes responsibility for providing a platform, the end users take responsibility for contributing effectively.

4 The minimum viable effort should be expended in getting things done.

5 Everything should be questioned, to avoid getting wrapped up in unnecessary actions.

6 Everybody works best in their own way, so give them freedom to act.

7 Great work is as much art as it is science. Allow people to express themselves.

8 Creativity comes from alternative perspectives. Human workplaces are structured to encourage these.

9 Creating room to think and act allows great ideas and innovations to emerge naturally.

10 Allowing great things to happen, rather than trying to force them to, will always be more powerful.

The actions people take at work not only define their contribution, but the direction and success of the business. Human organizations enable these by providing just enough structure and direction to guide actions, then getting out of the way and allowing them to happen. With creation, collaboration and sharing being so fundamental to this, the right communication and technology brings every aspect of a human organization together.

Task 6: brainstorming your action plan

This is a simple strategic exploration exercise to use in exploring opportunities, priorities and how to make them real. It can be used at any level from individual and team, to department, unit or even entire organization.

Take a large sheet of paper; maybe the entire size of a table top.

Brainstorm

On the paper, write the objective you would like to explore. This could be something like 'Create a more human workplace, or strategy for next 12 months'.

Spend some time (30 minutes is ideal) exploring all the ideas you have on the topic. Draw links between them, use images, notes, thoughts and highlight major ideas.

Once you're done, pin it to the wall.

Stand back and be objective

Look at all the ideas and what connects them. Try to pick out common themes and create a list of adjectives. Take two smaller sheets of paper and crunch the information from your thought process down into two lists:

1 *Three priorities.* What are the three key priorities your ideas have shown, that will take you towards your objective in the most effective or powerful way?

2 *Three immediate opportunities.* Within these priority areas, what are the three immediate opportunities for action that you can take to set the ball rolling and make progress towards your priorities and overall objective?

Once you have these, you can start applying some of the more in-depth tools from this chapter to take them forward.

Reference

Walker, M (2009) 'Evolution is slowing snails down', bbc.co.uk, 11 May. Available from: http://news.bbc.co.uk/earth/hi/earth_news/newsid_8043000/8043689.stm [Accessed 22 April 2017].

Communications 06 and technology

This is a short chapter. Not because comms and tech aren't important – quite the opposite! Because they are so important, decisions on how to manifest them can only be taken by the organization itself, within its own context, and those decisions are some of the most important the platform needs to make.

Often, communications and technology are referred to as infrastructure. They do contribute to the basic structures needed for the operation of an organization, but their role is deeper than that. They are the wrapper that binds the entire organization and community to the business, the glue that holds everything together.

This chapter explores:

- why comms and tech are important to unlocking a human workplace;
- how the right strategy underpins the community connection and enables better work;
- the idea that automation is not the enemy of the human workplace;
- ideas for considering the right approaches for your organization.

Not the answer (part of the question)

Organizations are made up of the right people, in the right places, doing the right things. The technology to create and support this, as well as the ability to flow the right information across the organization within the freedoms created by minimum viable structure, enables all of these things to happen.

Earlier we mentioned how without people there is no business, yet it's the combination of communication and the technology to support it that allows the organization to:

- *Identify the right people*
  By using communication, selection, engagement and data to create a filter that attracts well-aligned people to the human workplace and begins a conversation with them through an immersive positive experience.

- *Bring them into the community*
  Expanding the process as it moves through the filter to attract the right people towards the nucleus of the community with an effective two-way application and onboarding process.

- *Untether them from restrictive spaces*
  Offering a coherent, simple set of tools that enables collaboration, communication and flexible working. Whether allowing maximum working mobility through cloud systems and mobile tech, or supporting instant, productive conversations between colleagues on opposite sides of the world.

- *Unleash them to do their best work*
  Creating choice, freedom and enough of an offering to enable individuals and teams to work to their absolute best. This includes systems that work, intuitive software and productivity tools, without over-complication or overwhelming. Keep it coherent!

Without getting these things right, the organizational platform will work far less effectively and progress towards the business goal will be lost. Enablement of people is the cornerstone of a human workplace. Communication and technology make it possible. In themselves, they are not answers but services to be considered and implemented to underpin what's already there. The question remains for every organization – what do we need to enable our organizational platform?

Enabler of better things

The least successful modern organizations are those that see tech or comms as having the answer. They install systems and wait for people to change their behaviours and start using them, becoming confused when that doesn't happen. Unaware that the system is not the answer, just the enabler of something that's already there, they look to the system itself for answers.

I was told about a project to install an Enterprise Social Network (ESN) at a major global pharmaceutical company. It was implemented as a system and once live, the expectation was that conversation and collaboration would start. It didn't.

The organization wasn't encouraging collaborative, conversational behaviours, so there was nothing to drive towards the platform. It was only when they changed their viewpoint and realized that the ESN would be an outlet for the behaviours that they focused on people. Only a few months later, the adoption went from 0 to 50,000 users across the organization and it started to reap the benefits.

In a previous public sector role, I was implementing records tracking systems, which involved the shift from handwritten tracking records to instant traces via barcode scanning. In our first change management attempt, there was huge resistance to a new system. When we flipped the problem and focused on the benefits to the users and how it would improve their ability to do their best work, the resistance started to fall away and we launched successfully.

Both of these examples demonstrate that if you think of the solution before you think of the actual impact on the end users and the experience they will have using it, you will set up to fail. Whether structure, system, hardware or enabler, the only reason your human workplace should do anything is to benefit its community. If it doesn't do that, it has no purpose. Think of the ability to offer all workers flexibility around freedom within parameters. It's impossible to unleash a worker if the technology they use can't support it. I can't mobile work from a desk PC any more than I can do a stock check on an iPad in a warehouse with no WiFi. Equally, installing another piece of software that doesn't create positive impact on my work and attempting to force me to use it, will do nothing but turn me off and create a mini-rebellion.

Technology and communication systems help the organizational platform to provide the right services to the community, enabling individuals and teams to do their best work and supporting collaboration, creativity, innovation and insight through the flow of information. In themselves they are not the answer, but they enable the answer to happen. Their role is to enhance.

Building (not burning) bridges

The frustration that erupts when technology is inadequate, fails or is undersupported is tangible. I've spent time in many workplaces where aspirations of unleashing work outreach the actual capability for doing so:

- a creative agency with an expensive, agile workplace, where Wi-Fi was not available in all of the useable workspaces;

- a food production plant where the requirement to complete new paper-work in specific locations was made impossible by the environmental conditions;

- a recruiting company where the complex phone system put barriers to communication internally and externally, despite that being the corner-stone of the business.

If your aim is to create a community around a shared goal and enable it to pursue that goal, you need to give it the ability to do so. If you don't and people become frustrated, not only does the community become less functional, it can become harder to build and maintain the community. Organizations are made up of the right people, in the right places, taking the right actions, enabled by communication and technology. When any one of these things fails, it impacts another and as a knock-on effect, it *always* affects people. Poor IT support, or the wrong tech solutions can create more impact than just a few hours' downtime.

Make your mantra *enable, not block*. Design for people – there is no other reason.

Networks and communities

Your organization is a community of people, reaching outwards from a nucleus. At the centre, the connections between members are strongest and they vary as appropriate with each individual's involvement as the community radiates out.

Within the community, there are teams and collaborators, individuals and collectives. Each of these forms a sub-community in its own right and together within the community, they connect to form a network. Connection in the community of a human organization doesn't have to be linear. By free-ing the flow of information between any two (or more) points at any given time, the connections behave as a network within the community.

It may feel messy and out of control compared to the triangular top-down hierarchy of information previously prevalent and that's because in a way, it is. It needs to be. You can't get the right information between two places if it can't go direct. Equally, the right conversations can't happen if they are blocked. Look on free-flowing information as controlled chaos. By providing the right methods and channels for it to happen, it becomes useful as an enabler for your human workplace, without either blocking or spiralling into unusable chaos.

Don't worry, your organization isn't expected to control every single aspect of these information communities and networks (if anything, that could start to block their potential), just trust in their power. The world around us proves the influence and power of networks. They have brought governments down, brought new ones in, shown the real story beyond the 'official' message and even brought about the mainstream rise of fake news. They are powerful, but by enabling them through the shared drive of the community and its behaviours, an organization can put them to work to achieve its mission.

Wider still, each individual within the community and its reach has their own personal network. If they are empowered and inspired by their human workplace to share positive information and stories, the power of the organization's own reach is magnified to the nth degree. We've seen many examples of the power of organizational networks already, including:

- Schneider Electric creating a global drive for wellness through sharing information and ideas;
- Hershey recognizing its people through a peer-to-peer platform and unlocking the engagement and productivity benefits of doing so;
- Buffer remotely managing a global workforce, creating a coherent identity and driving success through technology and communication alone.

Don't fear the network, it's a powerful tool. These examples and the others in this book all give the community the right platform to thrive, through wrapping their other initiatives in well-intentioned, accessible and simple technology and communication approaches. Developing a human workplace in the right way allows good things to happen!

Automation is not your enemy

A final word on the ever-intensifying forward march of technology in the workplace ...

There's much talk, particularly in circles predicting the future of work, around automation. Books have been written on the subject, and governments are starting to consider the social and economic impacts of roles wiped out by automation.

In 2016 various news outlets reported how technology manufacturer Foxconn, which manufactures for Apple and Samsung had reduced its workforce by 60,000 workers due to the implementation of robots (Statt, 2016).

It's a concern on many levels, although this isn't the forum for a philosophical debate. A human workplace may actually thrive if it embraces automation, as it can allow its people to focus on things people do best. Also, the fundamental part of any business' community is that it's based on contribution. If you're unable to contribute, you're unable to remain in the community.

As harsh as this sounds, it's the same evolutionary factor that signals the warning alarms for organizations that are too traditional (or not human enough) to adapt to the changing world. If they are unable to adapt, they will fail. The world of work is a constant quest for relevance and that's something that policy makers and each of us as workers needs to take responsibility for.

Right now, human workplaces are using technology in amazing ways to further connect with their people and enable them to be their whole selves at work, interact, participate and contribute with a level of freedom they have never previously experienced. Some are even using automation to allow their organizational platform to free their people up to do the things that people do best.

To date, things humans can do that robots just can't come close to include:

- building relationships;
- caring;
- empathizing;
- creating.

Technology can enable and inform all of these things, but it can't actually do them as effectively as humans. It lacks the human-to-human connection that's required to do them well.

UK engineering company Matt Black Systems reduced its workforce by two-thirds by automating its back end administrative functions. Anything that was process driven – admin, accounting, human resource functions such as annual leave booking and absence recording – was amalgamated into a self-designed system. This freed the people to contribute to building relationships, delivering amazing service, troubleshooting and innovating. The community became smaller, but closer, while contributions increased due to the better connections in the organizational community.

Early in the book we looked at how perpetual growth and scale are not sustainable, offering human workplaces as an alternative perspective to combat this. Human workplaces aim to be *minimum viable organizations* which achieve through *minimum viable effort*, avoiding complexity and following their business goals as simply as possible in doing so. It's inevitable that automation, implemented for the right reasons, will be a solution that enhances the organization's ability to support the business.

If you're building a human workplace, automation is not your enemy. If you're a worker unable to adapt, it may just be. It's the evolve or die debate again, but from the other side of the coin. I know this is a contentious point and we've only scratched the surface here, but now is the right time for starting the conversation!

Ten key ideas on communications and technology for your human workplace

1 Technology in itself is not an answer, it's an enabler of answers.

2 Human workplaces are based on human connections, technology and communication are the glue that binds this all together.

3 Keeping it simple by providing the minimum viable amount of the right systems is essential.

4 Only do things where there is a clear purpose and benefit. People won't adopt what they have no reason to use.

5 To truly activate your business' community, view it as a network.

6 Information should be free to flow between any two points in the community, in a useful way, at any time.

7 The more control you place on the network, the more you block its effectiveness and prevent benefits like collaborative thinking and innovation from happening.

8 Some of the world's largest, most complex organizations are effectively harnessing the power of their internal networks to fuel people-first success.

9 Automation can help to create human workplaces, not just de-humanize.

10 The solution for your organization will be individual to it.

Binding the people, place and actions of your human workplace together with the right mix of communication and technology is not an option, but an imperative. These are the things enable the coherence and functioning of your community, harnessing its power by turning it into a network. As necessary as they are, their success hangs on one pivotal factor – adoption. The only way technology and communication can be successful and enable your human workplace is if your people actually use systems the organizational platform provides. Creating adoption is our next step.

Task 7: reviewing what you have

As technology and communications are what binds a human workplace together, a good place to start thinking about them is by reviewing what you already have. Using Figure 6.1, make a list of any systems and solutions you have in place for the key human workplace priority areas of people, place, action and also think of any others.

Once you have this picture of *what is now*, consider it using the questions posed in Figure 5.5 to start understanding how you could make your provision to your people simpler, better and more human.

Think about:

- duplication or any overlap there may be;
- unnecessary process or procedure that can be cut;
- what's missing;
- things that can be improved.

Once you're done, you have a basis for exploration. Chapter 5 will help you take it further!

Figure 6.1   Simple comms and tech assessment

PEOPLE	PLACE
ACTION	OTHER

Reference

Statt, N (2016) 'iPhone manufacturer Foxconn plans to replace almost every human worker with robots', *The Verge,* 30 December. Available from: www.theverge.com/2016/12/30/14128870/foxconn-robots-automation-apple-iphone-china-manufacturing [Accessed 23 April 2017].

Getting there: making the change

07

The ideas behind a human workplace are clear and the benefits are obvious. However they're structured, organizations that are able to move fluidly, not only to respond to the changing demands of the world, but to proactively connect with a community, are the ones that will win.

It's simple for a three-person startup to set itself in these ways, relatively easy for an organization with fewer than 50 people to do the same, but at higher numbers than these the dispersion of the community means maintaining the connection that's central to the whole idea becomes difficult.

The larger the scale, the more difficult it becomes. A global organization of 100,000 or more employees has a level of in-built complexity, regardless of how badly it wants to remove it. To reach that scale takes a huge amount of time too, so along the way, that organization will have inherited and ingrained many of the systems and structures that we're now seeing as outmoded.

Intention to change, company-wide resolutions and board-level strategies are fantastic, but it's action that really counts. Making your workplace human cannot be achieved by words; *something needs to happen*, even where the task in hand seems insurmountable.

That's what this chapter is about.

This chapter explores:

- how to drive adoption through seeding and spreading ideas;
- inspiring organizational change through people;
- Discover – Imagine – Create: a method for making change human;
- how positive activism can be your secret weapon;
- why this is a natural manifestation of the human workplace mindset.

Making it real

A large part of my work is creating transition programmes and I spend much of my time studying what makes change successful, but also the benefits of making it human. As change maker for BDG architecture + design, I design and implement workplace and organizational change for organizations of all sizes, scales and levels of complexity, helping to connect people with their work, workplace, organization and each other. We'll use my approach as the framework for this chapter.

Seed and spread ideas

Any kind of change affects people. We're creatures of habit and our behaviours are ingrained through endless repetition and practice. They become *normal*. When normal becomes different, however positive or beneficial the looming changes may be, they pose a threat to what we know, so many of us naturally view them with suspicion. We create barriers that protect our current view of normal.

That's a generalization – people view change in a number of different ways. How they view change impacts how ready they are to adopt and adapt to it. This forms a powerful tool in driving change through an organization at any scale.

The three starting viewpoints when faced with impending change are:

1 *Champions*
   Proactively positive about the change. Potential evangelists who are not only ready to adopt and adapt to the change, but actively share that positivity with others. *Evangelists* are the most powerful champions, most likely to demonstrate positive activism in support of the change.

2 *Fence sitters*
   Understand the potential positive elements of the change, but are happy as they are, doing things the way they have always done them.

3 *Blockers*
   Against the change, because they want things to stay as they are, or believe the change will be a bad thing. Within this group there are two types of blocker:

   - passive blockers are not in favour of the change and will drag their heels through the process;
   - active blockers will deliberately try to sabotage or disrupt the change.

Successful change is the *successful adoption of a new idea*. Refer back to the adoption curve that we saw in Figure 2.6. Since any change involves the introduction of new ideas into the community, it applies in the same way. Evangelists and champions are the positive activists and promoters of the idea, fence sitters are the majority whose stance shifts the weight of popular opinion beyond the tipping point and blockers are both those who will never be convinced and those who actively try to prevent change. The aim of any change is to have the new idea positively adopted and see people's behaviours and habits adapt to make that happen. It's a question of moving it through the adoption curve.

While you could focus all your energy on the blockers, as they are the ones with the furthest distance to go, moving through the adoption curve is actually about the weight of popular opinion. If you can bring positive popular opinion over the 50 per cent mark, it starts to outweigh the negative, creating a snowball effect and overwhelming any remaining negativity.

As the weight of opinion moves in favour of positive adoption, it dilutes the noise coming from the blockers and lessens the potential impact of active blocking. There will always be active blockers and they will always be the last to be convinced that a change is positive – often they will leave the organization before adopting it. That's just fine.

Focusing your efforts on changing the opinion of blockers is a waste of time and resources, because if their viewpoint cannot become positive, then they become the wrong people for the organization at that time and unable to play a further part in the community. If you can outweigh blocker negativity with positivity loudly enough, they become inconsequential in the grand scheme of wider adoption anyway, giving you time and space to move them within or out of the community.

To create the positive momentum that drives adoption, you need to *seed and spread ideas*. Although exact ratios of opinion vary with every change, typically the starting point will appear as shown in Figure 7.1.

Figure 7.1 Seeding and spreading ideas: starting point

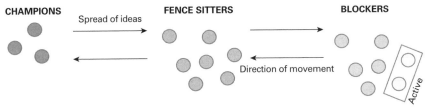

Figure 7.2   Seeding and spreading ideas: outcome

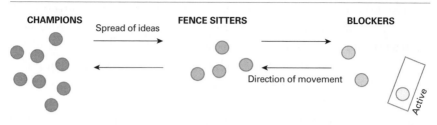

To move through the adoption curve and take popular opinion into the majority, you need to start moving fence sitters to the champion viewpoint and passive blockers to fence sitters (once they are there, they are easier to turn into champions). The most effective way to do this is by *using the champions as evangelists* who amplify the message and are more connected with their peers than messages broadcast from the top.

If they are enabled to *own the change* and take an active role in seeing the successful adoption of something they believe in, people will help to spread the ideas. By seeding the positive story of the change into everyone, with a focus on those who already view it positively, it's possible to spread positivity and start shifting people's viewpoints.

When you can make that happen, you can shift the weight of opinion in favour of the change, as shown in Figure 7.2.

Of course, the earlier you do this in the change process, the earlier you'll achieve critical mass on positive adoption. That's why it's important to not only invest in creating change, but in driving its adoption, because that's how you secure the investment in doing something differently.

If you invest in something different, deliver it and fail to connect it with the people it impacts, you'll be fire fighting – trying to connect people and force adoption after it goes live. In the long run that will cost more in time, money and missed opportunity than it would to recognize the connection between change and people upfront, and do something about it.

Approaches to driving change

Top-down change

You could approach change from the top, as a business transformation project. This is where senior leadership decides something is going to happen, then launches a project to filter it down through the organization via broadcast communication, before launching a process of engagement.

Figure 7.3   Restricted idea flow

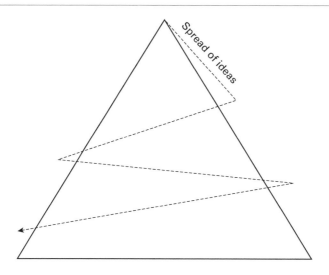

Figure 7.4   Old fashioned linear change management

Here, ideas spread as in Figure 7.3. This is expensive and slow. It also carries the risk that by dictating a change, the people it impacts are alienated and not given ownership to drive positive adoption. To achieve success with this approach requires a lot of time, money and effort to get the adoption curve to critical positive mass. What this often looks like is an increasingly outdated linear version of change management that offers tokenistic information, as shown in Figure 7.4.

This is a linear approach that takes defined starting and ending points. It assumes that giving people the information needed to understand the shift in between (communication and training) is all it takes. That's not usually the case.

Right at the very start, we looked at how business is no longer linear; it's a series of ever-evolving cycles. Any change is part of that evolution. It's not an isolated project, it's a cycle that continues and fits into a larger evolutionary cycle. *Change in the modern organization is never complete* and likewise, supporting its adoptions should be continuous. People are affected by change and need to be connected with it.

The creation of a new physical workplace doesn't stop as soon as the last worker moves in; it continues to evolve forever within the changing working needs of the organization and people.

The implementation of a piece of software can change the way people work. Once they are connected to it and adopt it, this may impact their demands of the workspace, which will need further evolution.

Everything impacts everything else.

Free-range change

An alternative approach (and the most effective and impactful), is to seed and spread ideas from wherever the champions lie within the organization. This way provides ownership to the people and acts as *peer-to-peer spreading*, rather than broadcast dictation. It's the way we see information and trends seeding and spreading in the world outside the workplace, so why should we think human behaviour is any different just because it is in the workplace?

People are people, whether at work or not, allowing them to behave as naturally as possible is the simplest way to create a connection. This natural spread of ideas is more rapid and more effective, giving everyone the opportunity for a positive, personal connection with the change.

Here, ideas spread as visualized in Figure 7.5.

Compare this with Figure 2.1 and you can see that this uses the community and network to spread ideas. If success is defined by majority positive adoption, then *this approach is always the most effective*. Because champions

Figure 7.5   Free-range change

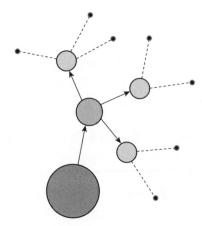

each act as a nucleus for a change cell, they radiate positive adoption. This happens simultaneously in different parts of the organization, amplifying every time a fence sitter becomes a champion.

It may seem more random and chaotic, but just as with the free flow of information around the organization it's more powerful in driving towards the absolute aim of achieving majority positive opinion. It can be a more cost-effective way to approach change, too.

Of course, there need to be champions in the first place. But if you're unable to find them, it means what you're trying to do is not perceived as positive, or owned by your people. My first major change project in health-care used change champions who were employed for that reason. Their message lacked authenticity and it became even harder to identify positive adopters across the organization, ultimately affecting the successful implementation of the project. No amount of top-down message broadcasting will alter that and the change will fail. Unless something is done for the right reasons, it will never work!

Political barriers

The more complex an organization is, the more politics play a part in blocking progress. Opportunities are lost daily by the application of unnecessary rules and restrictions for various reasons. Sometimes it's people doing their jobs, sometimes it's people protecting their interests. Every time it's due to negative, restrictive human behaviour.

In human workplaces, people are trusted to take the right actions and act in the interests of the common goal. To do that takes two things: freedom and trust.

If the organization isn't set up to trust its people and offer them freedom within parameters, then people won't trust each other. That means the organizational platform is broken. When personal purpose becomes an in-work agenda, it's an issue. It's also a sign that the organization has the wrong people, or is set-up to allow them to take the wrong actions.

There are some fundamental barriers to remove to open up freedom and trust in the way required to eliminate as much politics as possible. For example, in complex organizations where individual units have their own profit and loss accounts, the idea of letting a member of their team collaborate on a piece of work somewhere else in the business without formalizing a budgetary recharge is unthinkable, because this represents use of their resources and affects their profit and loss.

There are so many equivalents to this – examples I've encountered in major organizations (but would be unfair to list here), which restrict them from progressing and prevent them from taking opportunities. Cross-department collaboration restrictions, perceived threat to management status, fear of openness – all are common, all are avoidable. Such unnecessary restrictions even prevented potential contributors to this book sharing the amazing things they are doing in the name of their businesses.

It's unnecessary and counter intuitive and an example of the lack of trust and freedom to act that still exists in organizations of all shapes and sizes. This ingrained *organizational blocking needs to be removed* from the system if individuals are to really take ownership and drive a successful future. The organizational platform must be designed and operated around freedom within parameters.

Encouraging positive behaviour is a *positive* approach. Applying restrictions is a *negative* one.

Internal politics is the manifestation of a broken system. Take an honest look at your organization and ask if it's blocking its people (or allowing them to be blocked). If it is, it's blocking its own progress.

Why change is important

There are many people who will tell you that change management is dead. It's not. Our understanding of it is changing so that it is seen to be less a linear one-off project, so much as an ongoing, ingrained part of an organization.

If our organizations are fluid and the platform constantly evolving, attention to bringing the people along with the change is essential. It's part of helping them to take the right actions. Individual programmes are still needed when a big leap happens – like the move from one workstyle to another – but they aren't in isolation. The rise of internal communications is a demonstration of this emergence of organizations starting to realize this.

An organization's ability to change is its ability to fit the shifting world around it. That makes it the most important aspect of the human workplace, because for all the great conversations about ideas and possibilities, the only organizations that can ever get there are the ones that somehow get themselves over the line – a line that's continually shifting.

To transform a complex, structured, dispersed or set-in-its ways organization into an agile, lean, fluid community built around the strong nucleus of a single, well-defined mission may seem difficult. In all honesty, it should be!

Nothing worthwhile ever comes easy, but it's how we approach the transition that really matters. The responsibility for making an amazing human workplace rests with everyone. It's not up to the CEO to drive it, or up to any other specific individual (although they can all assume a share of responsibility). It's up to everyone – if you really want it to happen, set the wheels in motion.

To understand how to get started and how to start to move towards, as well as reap the benefits of, becoming a human workplace, we need to go right back to the beginning. Becoming a human workplace is no single project, with an A to B defined start and finish point, it's a journey that never ends.

We live in an age of evolution. Human workplaces are that in evidence and there are some simple, powerful things anyone can do to get started. The only reason *why* is because you believe in better.

Change as evolution

When an organization realizes it's in a constant state of change, it can allow for that within its platform. Rather than the A to B of old-fashioned organizational change and development, it can create an open, participatory system driven by the unleashed flow of information and communication. In short, purely through the way it operates, it can give people ownership of any change by doing things for the right reasons and giving them real context.

Rather than a line of individual, isolated projects, it's a series of circles. It's not imposed change, it's owned change, spread through the organizational community from a vocal base of Champions. It's nuclear change.

Before undertaking any organizational change, there are some very basic questions to ask.

Change checklist

- *Reasons.* Is it for the right reasons?
- *Reaction.* How will the community react initially?
- *Champions.* Who are the champions that really believe in this?
- *Bigger picture.* How does it fit in to the organizational context?
- *Parameters.* What are the timescales and other immovable factors that must be taken into account?

Start small

The further away your starting point is from where you want to be, the more daunting the journey to it seems to be. Moving from fixed desk, fixed hours to fully flexible working across an entire organization is a major undertaking. It's probably too major to attempt as a single leap.

By looking at organizational development as an evolution, there is no expectation to do everything in one go. Not only would it be too difficult, the end goal may have moved on by the time you get there.

Our organizations are in perpetual beta, which means that at all times they are the minimum viable version of themselves and constantly developing based on feedback from their users. It's design thinking in practice:

1 *Understand*. The real need, or reason here.

2 *Think*. Take user insight to develop a perspective.

3 *Design*. Create a solution.

4 *Make*. Prototype that solution.

5 *Test*. Pilot it in a small segment of the organization.

By working through these stages and at a small scale, if something is wrong, you can move back to any of the previous stages to solve and tweak. Iterating your solution based on real user insight gained through engaging with people (through open conversation, surveys or any other method) is the most powerful way of making a connection with them. *When people connect, they adopt.*

This is the essence of seeding and spreading ideas. Engage people in designing the solution, prove it works, then roll it out increasingly widely and iterate as you go.

It's an active quality filter that continuously improves everything you do. By placing the wheels in motion you create a consistent forward trajectory, rather than the rapid dump of a top-down change enforcement. Every small success in the evolutionary cycle helps build some more momentum. Every small failure helps reiterate, rather than off-road the entire change. There's a knock-on effect, too. If something good happens, tests well and is celebrated, it can start to organically reach the rest of the organization. With some proactive help from the organizational platform, it becomes adopted as part of the platform itself.

All it takes is an evolutionary approach and some protagonists of positive change. These champions can be anyone. Positive change can be seeded from anywhere in the organization. It's how it spread that defines its long-term success. Origin seeds can come from:

- a strategic, platform-driven movement, such as senior leadership or organizational development teams;
- local practical initiatives leading the way (locations, units, departments);
- teams of collaborators (coming together in any way – if you let them connect they will form);
- an individual who believes and has the freedom or courage to act.

Like permission, responsibility can be given, but it can also be taken. If people adopt a mindset where they are able to try things, they will. The outliers are where the power is – the rebels *with* a cause. The people who have the strongest connection with the organizational community believe in the business mission and are unleashed to act freely in its interest, naturally strive for positive change with the benefit of the business in mind. They do the right things for the right reasons, because they are unleashed to do so.

Global strategy, local implementation

The real insight in any organization is with the people at all levels of the community, at all proximities from the nucleus. Creating an organization-wide strategy is a great idea for coherence, but trying implement a strategy as a one-for-all single global solution is disruptive (and not in a good startup way).

The larger and more complex the organization is, the more destructive it becomes to attempt to impose a one size fits all solution. It just doesn't make sense to force a single answer on to a range of contexts. Just like great art, great organizations are developed through conceptual interpretation.

Even if it could be done effectively, the time it takes to roll an idea out across the world means it's outmoded at the start by the time it arrives at the end – a bit like painting the Golden Gate Bridge.

Creating strategies, then allowing freedom to act to interpret and apply them locally is sensible, if for no other reason than the contextual factors that influence and impact at the local level:

- geography;
- local culture;
- workstyles;
- preferences;
- needs.

As we've seen from unleashing the flow of information in organizations, insight and knowledge is at its greatest where the work happens.

Understanding the local context is an essential part of putting the platform in the hands of the people it needs to enable. It allows them to successfully adapt a global strategy into something sustainably deliverable on a local level.

You can't apply something designed a thousand miles away in a completely different contextual setting, but you can create a set of guidelines in keeping with the organizational platform that can be used for local adaptation. The more ownership you can place in the hands of the community at the point of impact, the faster ideas seed, spread and are adopted.

Almost every case study we've seen in this book highlights how the organization has succeeded through adopting this global strategy, local implementation approach. From LEGO with workplace design, to Hershey with recognition, CGI with organizational structure and workplace change at SAP. It's a common thread that combines coherence with ownership to great effect.

The art of the organization

Don't assume that everything about developing an organization is a science. It's great when things can be logical and measurable, but there's a huge value to allowing things to be artistic and creative. It's not so easy to measure these approaches, but it allows work to become a performance and connect with people emotionally. Creating a human workplace isn't science, it's art.

It's a deeper, human connection as opposed to an instantly measurable transaction and one that's completely at odds with traditional business thinking. Scientific process works well for A to B, linear thinking. Artistic thinking allows for *interpretation, improvisation, exploration and alternative perspectives*. In a world of fluidity, that's a far more valuable mindset to employ.

CASE STUDY

The artistic workplace: interview with James Burke

Acrylicize is a creative practice that fuses art and design to explore identity. Their workplace installations not only create stimulating environments that unleash thought, they connect people with the essence of the organization or brand, becoming a major part of the workplace user experience. Creative director and founder James Burke shared his thoughts on workplace creativity.

What makes a creative workplace

The ability to collaborate within an open and friendly culture – one embedded in trust, where people feel that they are able to give forward their ideas no matter how good, bad or ugly. This creates a rich environment for innovation to surface as most of the time you have to go through a few bad ideas to get a good one. If you feel you can go on the journey safely you're more likely to get to the gold.

In practical terms, having the tools at your disposal to encourage those moments of inspiration is crucial. Things like walls that you can draw over, a library of inspiration that takes you away from your computer and into a quiet space, as well as opportunities for people to gather, discuss and collaborate always help.

For me it's about making a place as fun as engaging as possible. When we work in this type of environment we tend to do our best stuff. Investing in the workplace where we spend most of our day means ultimately we are happier in our work. This can only lead to better wellbeing for staff and better results for an organization.

What art in the workplace means

Art has the power to articulate a story in a way unlike anything else. The ability to distil a thought into a single moment that requires contemplation and reflection is what makes it so powerful.

If an organization invests in art, I think it sends out a message that there is a commitment to creativity and a real sense of pride and identity within their space.

Practising what you preach

Acrylicize was born out of art school and when I came to the end of my degree I really wasn't ready to finish my project – I felt like I was only just getting started. What really inspired me about the environment of art school was the concept of the shared studio space. An environment rich in creative energy, designed solely for people to create, do their thing and be inspired by everyone else around them.

I loved that people would naturally critique each other's work, vibe off each other and ultimately push each other forward by offering different views and perspectives. This is what I want to capture and bring to workplaces.

Our own story has always been very organic. What I set out to do at the beginning and what we now do as a studio has been a very fluid process. We take each step at a time, learning where we can, living in the present moment. We use the same process for our clients.

Creativity is a process, you don't need to know where you're going to end up when you start out. You just need to make a move, take a positive step and then work out each play as it unfolds in front of you.

This principle of constant questioning allows organizations to explore their identities, in our case using art and design to articulate concepts of personal spirit, unique stories and individual DNA.

Three tips for creating inspiration in the workplace

1 *Give people a say*
   If people feel they have a sense of ownership they are much more likely to engage and take responsibility.

2 *Create opportunities for collaboration*
   Whether working or socializing, by coming together to share, colleagues get to know each better, allowing them to connect more deeply around their work.

3 *Lead by example*
   If the workforce sees the leadership living out company beliefs and codes honestly and truthfully then this sets the example to the rest of the company. A bunch of rules that look good on paper but aren't practised by the very people running the company are very unlikely to make any kind of meaningful impact.

The price of change

Doing things costs money. Getting them wrong costs even more.

An all-out top-down business transformation is not only hugely expensive and time consuming, but takes significant additional investment per individual to do the work required to create the connection between people and change. In my experience working on such programmes, this cost is in the region of around $1,000–1,500 per individual and that doesn't include the cost of removing those who are no longer the right people from the organization. It's a huge undertaking.

There's no doubt that for the right reasons, an all-out business transformation is a powerful thing, but does your business have the cash to do that? Investing in people always reaps rewards. In a company that has $1 billion of annual revenue, a 4 per cent increase in revenue from a $10,000,000 investment in transformation makes financial sense – it's a 4:1 return on the investment. There are many good programmes that have shown this to be deliverable and focus across the board on people, place and action to bring an organization into the future.

Such programmes are comprehensive, immersive and above all, effective. But that programme of work comes at a financial and time cost. Often it's the organizations most in need of change, that are least able to afford it, or least able to see it and adopt it as a top-down approach. Where that's the case, change, transition, transformation or whatever you want to call it is still possible, but it's an evolution rather than a revolution. Gradual *free-range change* balanced with the *design thinking mindset* is the key.

It's a more cost-effective, gradual, smoother and less-intrusive way to seed and spread ideas. It's organic, against its more expensive, intensive counterpart approach. Both work; but one is far more expensive than the other. As long as your pace of change is constantly enabling people to do their best work and the business to pursue its goals with the fewest possible obstacles, your approach is working.

Making change human

Every business exists to succeed, whatever that individual definition of success might be. Enabling that success is why our organizations exist, too. No one ever set up a business to fail and no one ever deliberately changed a part of their organizational platform in order to fail.

Anything we do within our organizations should be aimed at contributing to that success. If it's not, there's no reason to do it (so it shouldn't be done). The drive for success is why we create change within our organizations. Our attempts to improve aspects of our platform to better pursue our goals are what *change* is. That's what needs to be managed.

To understand what we need to change and when, we need to have a clear picture of what success looks like for our own organization. If we know that, we can act for the right reason and pursue it. Any other reason is wrong – and there are many misguided change-related projects and programmes out there. Here are my top three examples:

- NHS electronic patient record: £4 billion overspent, never launched (*Guardian*, 2013).
- The Motorola Iridium Project: a £3 billion satellite-based mobile phone network that was technologically outdated before it ever launched (*The Independent*, 1999).
- Borders and the failure to adapt: with a lack of understanding of the changing world around it, Borders failed to adapt and continued doing what it always had. It was liquidated in 2011 (*Business Insider*, 2011).

All of these examples failed to really understand not only what to change and when to change it, but what people really wanted or needed from them.

They had no connection with their communities and were unable to adapt to the world around them.

Question: Does everyone in your organization share the same view of what success is?

When change fails

The statistics around organizational change are staggering: 70 per cent of change programmes fail (McKinsey, 2008). These are the reasons why:

- 39 per cent employee resistance;
- 33 per cent management behaviour;
- 14 per cent resource/budget;
- 14 per cent other reasons.

It's clear that, in the main, change projects are well-resourced and backed by the business. What causes them to fail is people! We're creatures of habit and by failing to recognize the impact of change on people, we expose ourselves to the risk of failing.

All change is an investment in one of two things: 1) business outcomes; 2) people.

It's very easy to focus on the business outcomes, by fully resourcing and supporting a change project in itself. This involves tangible figures and is simple to measure, so it fits with a traditional business viewpoint. The connection between change and people is much fluffier, but the stats show that this is the area that contributes most to the success or failure of a project.

Change can have a positive or negative knock-on effect on each of these things:

- people;
- place;
- action;
- technology;
- communication.

When you change one, you impact another. For example, the implementation of a new instant messaging software impacts the way people in the community communicate. A new flexible work*place* changes the way *people* work (*action*). There is no isolated change, which is why change projects can't be seen as one-off A to B exercises. They need to be seen in context.

The most important part of that context is people, because a change in any of the above areas will always impact people. People are the one common variable, they are also the most complex part of any organization and it's why failing to understand change as an investment in people and approaching it in a way that addresses that impact to combat employee resistance and poor management behaviour will always be inadequate.

The people variable

Every community is made up of individuals. Each of us experiences our relationship with the community in a unique, personal way and so we're affected by the impact of change in our own way. To successfully adopt change, it needs to connect with individuals and give them a reason to adopt it. To positively adopt any change, individuals need to change their own behaviours and habits. These things die hard and it's here that resistance arises.

I often share this true story, although I change the names and would never mention the business it happened in, purely because it happens everywhere, all the time.

Our workplaces are based on a series of relationships, as all communities are. Understanding how people connect with each other helps them to understand how they can connect with change. The enhancements to their behaviours and habits need to be demonstrated, to encourage adoption. Every change creates impact individually and collectively – in identity, as well as behaviour. What defines a team, how they collaborate, what lines exist and which are removed are all part of the impact and to enable people to adopt a change, they need support to adapt.

Bob and Kathy have both worked at the same company for many years. Each morning at 11 am precisely, Bob walks to the coffee machine. To get there, he passes Kathy's desk and they stop to chat. It's an enjoyable, social part of both of their days and has helped them in their work too through exchanging ideas.

When their company moved to a flexible workplace, both Bob and Kathy resisted the change. Bob in particular was vocal in his dissent and actively went out of his way to find issues and undermine the functioning of the new office. One day, when complaining about the bins not being emptied as often as in the old workplace (even though they were), a conversation with his manager allowed Bob to vent his true problem honestly.

The coffee machine had moved and nobody had a fixed desk anymore. As a result, not only did Bob not walk past Kathy en route to his morning caffeine fix, he didn't even know where to find her in the building. She could be anywhere! As a result, the quality of his experience in the workplace had suffered.

During the change, an instant messaging system had been put in place, but Bob had only been shown this is training. No direct connection between Bob and the change had been made, to demonstrate to him how the new workplace would enhance his habits and behaviours, rather than disrupt them negatively.

By using the instant messaging system, Bob was able to keep his interaction with Kathy going, find out where she was and arrange to meet and take time for an occasional coffee. When Bob was given reason to adapt and adopt the change, it enhanced his experience, but to do that, the personal connection with him needed to be made.

Making change work

Just like with the creative explorations we looked at in Chapter 5, any change should start with the question *What If …*

Unless there is a curiosity to understand the possibilities of doing things differently, there will be no exploration of the *who, what, where, why* and *how* of the impacts that doing this thing will cause. Exploration leads to understanding. When we understand things, we can start to visualize them and that starts the path to adoption. We can't move from one place to another without going on a journey. That journey is what determines successful change adoption. Bringing people along for the ride, rather than just delivering them to the final destination is where the trick lies.

Discover – Imagine – Create

BDG architecture + design creates workplaces for people. Before creating those places, the workplace strategy team gathers data to inform the design. Alongside much technical space utilization and other data, this includes gaining an understanding of:

- the organization;
- who its people are;

- how they work;
- how they could work;
- their attitude and readiness for change.

My role in all of this is to create the programme that connects the people with their work, workplace, organization and each other, as the change comes into effect; because, no matter how prepared people are, they need to be taken on the journey. We're creatures of habit, impacted individually and collectively by things changing, so we need a *level of reassurance* to convince us to adopt change. Just like people need to be connected with the business and community they work in and around, they need to be connected with the changes that impact them.

TOOL Discover – Imagine – Create

Taking people on a journey, not just teleporting them from place to place, needs exploration. Within the context of themselves and their organization, people need to:

- *Discover* the best of what is.
- *Imagine* what could be.
- *Create* the future together by making it real.

It's a simple journey, but by using it as a framework it allows people to tell their emerging story. They are real players, not just passengers. What that looks like needs to vary by organization, context and the actual facts of the change itself. But by leading people through a journey, allowing them to explore and see themselves and their work through a new lens, you can offer people the foundation for acceptance or adoption of any change – provided it's done for the right reasons in the first place!

How it works

Discovering the best of your work away from the context of your day-to-day habits and behaviours allows you to create a new perspective on what you do and how you do it. Ownership of the 'doing' part of your role in the organizational community, rather than the rituals you have placed around them, creates an objective detachment and openness to alternatives. Gathering alternative perspectives to complement your own allows for creative exploration and creates fertile ground for a mindset shift.

Global change communication programmes are one thing, but change affects us more personally as individuals, so must be addressed in that way, by allowing us to explore. Immersion, as we've already seen, is a driver of creativity and innovative thinking, so is the key to that exploration. Nearly all change programmes focus on perceived benefits, or the reasons a programme was designed. Giving those affected an opportunity for more abstract exploration, gives them the chance to discover more personal benefits that are otherwise unwritten.

Relationships are key to all communities, so creating space for collaboration and rethinking how everything could look and feel, with the right stimulus for thought, creates an imaginative reassessment of how things work. Underlying tensions and fears are allowed to emerge in a safe environment without judgement, when imaginative exploration is encouraged.

Linking this reassessed, rethought view of personal and collective behaviours and habits to the new context is the final opportunity. Exploring how to make things real, or replicate specific behaviours in a new setting seeds ideas around positive adoption. Spreading them through the community by creating an environment of celebration adds further momentum and pushes the positivity up through the adoption curve.

It's a simple approach that can be adapted for any change!

Five steps to success

Turning Discover – Imagine – Create into a programme of work that meets time, budget and scale requirements is only slightly more challenging. It's part psychology, part sociology, part creativity.

At BDG, we create stages that align with the overall project that is ushering in the change, flexing the programme to meet the needs of those affected as we travel the journey with them.

These are the stages of the journey:

1 *Prepare*
   Being well prepared by building a picture of everything related to the change. What it is, who it affects, why it's happening, timescales, stakeholders, project teams, champions.

2 *Inform*
   Involving everyone in the process by establishing open, clear lines of communication, opportunities for two-way feedback and creating touch points.

3 *Engage*
   Creating universal ownership through a programme of explorations, events and communications. Spreading ideas in collaboration with your champions.

4 *Reframe*

Creating new and different perspectives on every aspect of the change, with personal explorations of impact on behaviour and habits, while starting to connect them to the change.

5 *Inspire*

Foster a sense of celebration, positivity and ongoing communication around the change. Make sure it doesn't stop once the basic change has happened – that's just the beginning!

Using these stages to create the *minimum viable framework* for the journey, allows a programme of participation and immersion to be created that takes people along for the ride, as owners, not passengers. Look on these as the waypoints of the journey and build a programme that fits your business, your organization and your people.

Five tips for creating positive adoption

In any instance of organizational change, there are five golden rules I've come to learn drive success.

1 *Put people first*

Whatever you're changing, it will impact people either directly or as a knock-on effect. The more effective your people are, the more effective your organization is. Ensuring that whatever happens, your people can be their most effective is an absolute no-brainer, for those reasons.

2 *Consider the impact*

Whatever you're doing and whatever is driving it, look at the potential impact from all angles. What may deliver strategic benefits may also impact negatively on morale or capability. Make sure you cover every angle, because negative impact will hinder your organization's ability to work effectively.

3 *Ownership for all*

Because people are necessarily part of every possible organizational change, by virtue of being impacted by it, they need to be allowed to play that part. Of course, waiting for 100 per cent approval of every idea or action would mean nothing ever gets done, but ownership can be fostered through openness and making people feel included. It can be as simple as creating a forum for questions and feedback, or as in-depth as creating a personalized change journey.

Effective change is co-created; it will only be destructive if it's imposed.

4 *Communicate*

Keep everyone in the loop at all times. If you're doing the right thing for the right reason, there is never anything to hide. If you have something to hide, you're already going wrong. No problem ever got smaller by keeping it quiet until the unavoidable last moment!

5 *Think differently*
Approaching change in the same way as everyone else will never work. It needs to be your approach for your situation. Just like building organizations, creating workplaces or having ideas, your uniqueness is your secret weapon, but only you know how to operate it effectively!

All of these ideas can be used to drive change whether it comes from a positive or negative place. After all, a reduction in headcount is doing something for the right reason, if it saves the business.

Positive activism

Permission is a big word in all of this. Whether responsibility is given or taken, it's needed if anything is to ever happen. Traditionally, organizational development and change is led from the top, but what if a worker can see a positive impact or change that they could create and drive from their position in the organization. Why shouldn't they be empowered to do it? More importantly, why shouldn't they get on with it instantly?

If something is done for the right reasons – in the interest of the business and within the freedom within parameters framework, it can never be wrong. It needs those brave enough to take responsibility to drive real organizational change, because not only are they creating positive impact, they're proving that in any form of organizational structure, it's possible to achieve progress, regardless of where you sit in the hierarchy.

Doug Shaw is a friend of mine. He's an organizational development consultant and artist, doing some great work in this area. Doug wears a t-shirt that says *Proceed Until Apprehended*. It's a great message to anyone who believes something should be different: *Don't wait until you're told you're allowed to do it. Get on and make it happen.* If you're doing the right things for the right reasons, you will always be in the right. There are many stories I've encountered in organizations of all sizes where people have taken the initiative to pursue action for the benefit of the business, often putting their own jobs on the line in the process. If they had waited for permission to act, none of it would ever have happened.

This *act now, apologize later* approach is in keeping with design thinking as a fluid, adaptive approach to building organizations, but it needs participation. Positive activism of this sort should not only be allowed to flourish in an organization, but encouraged and celebrated as part of a dynamic step towards the future.

If all people in an organization are enabled as *positive activists*, they can choose where they are inspired to act. If the organizational platform enables them in the right way, positive activism will powerfully help to shape its future development and carry the business forward. Positive activists create rapid change; they drive non-linear business and are the key to your future. *Unleash them!*

Evolution through revolution

The evolution of an organization doesn't need to be driven by full-scale overhaul, but it does require revolutionary spirit. By unleashing people to contribute, act and adapt, the *power of the crowd* can be used to shape the future, driven by real-world insight from the community. Allowing, unleashing or just encouraging revolutionary spirit enables positive activism to emerge and organizational development to start to drive itself, following design thinking principles and always in the best interests of the organization.

The role for leadership and organizational development professionals is to *stand back and let it happen*. Create the platform. Positive activism, revolutionary change, unleashing people, removing structure. All of these things can seem daunting, particularly from a traditional linear point of view, as they could potentially expose the business to something that backfires. It takes some risk, but doing nothing and keeping things the way they have always been is the biggest risk an organization can take. Because in a crazy, unpredictable, fluid world, any organization that stands still too long and is unable to connect with its wider community, will be left behind. The risk of doing nothing is far worse than the risk of allowing people to act in good faith. Good communication and the constant flow of information keeps everything in public beta, allowing the entire community to provide feedback and influence progress.

A successful human workplace is about *ownership*. Making it happen is about crowdsourcing the future, via those who catalyse it. These workplaces aren't owned spaces for people to be grateful for their opportunity; they are platforms designed with people in mind. Because *when people thrive, organizations thrive too!*

Ten key ideas on making your human workplace real

1   Ideas can seed and spread in your organization, with adoption much like products in the consumer world.

2   Effectively creating change isn't about broadcasting messages, it's about taking people on the journey.

3   Using a design thinking approach to pilot projects is effective.

4   Driving change through giving people ownership increases adoption.

5   Creating change starts with an exploration, just like any creative approach.

6   There are simple ways to drive positive adoption through people.

7   Allowing people freedom to act can create major impact.

8   Unleashing positive activism is an opportunity.

9   Human workplaces are built on revolutionary spirit.

10 Giving people ownership is the most powerful tool of all.

Making your organization more human takes nothing more than building it people-first. To get there, it makes complete sense that any changes should be made with people at the centre of the process. Any organizational change is part of the story that everyone in your organization is creating together and it continues to be written every single day. That's why human workplaces, through design thinking, are adaptive and constantly responding to the world around them. They are always writing the next page of their exciting, collaborative story.

Task 8: introduction to Discover – Imagine – Create

As a method of driving adoption by taking people on a journey and telling a story, this is really powerful. Without expecting you to build a whole programme around it, let's introduce the concepts by thinking about an area in your organization you might like to rethink.

Work this through on a piece of paper, or on a screen.

- *Heading*
  What are you investigating?

- *Discover*
  Define what great looks like in this instance. How do you know when it's going well, what does it feel like, what happens? Explore the best of what is, by removing the connection with place and habits and really getting to the essence of what makes great.

- *Imagine*
  Think how great could be delivered in completely new ways, unconfined by the restrictions of current behaviours, habits, systems, procedures and environments. Use some of the creative thinking techniques from Chapter 5, if you like.

- *Create*
  Think about how to make this new perspective of great real in a way that's actually deliverable. Tether it back to the real world with a list of initiatives or changes that would be needed to make it happen.

You now have a new perspective and the basis of an action plan. Over to you to make the change real!

References

Johnson, D (2011) '2 big companies that missed the opportunity to adapt to new technology', 28 November. Available from: www.businessinsider.com/overcome-by-change-the-failure-of-two-companies-to-seize-the-initiative-and-master-oncoming-change-2011-11?IR=T [Accessed 23 April 2017].

McIntosh, B (1999) 'Down to earth reasons for Iridium failure', *The Independent*, 18 August. Available from: www.independent.co.uk/news/business/down-to-earth-reasons-for-iridium-failure-1113638.html [Accessed 23 April 2017].

McKinsey (2008) 'Quarterly transformation executive survey'. Summary available from www.slideshare.net/aipmm/70-26633757 [Accessed 23 April 2017].

Syal, R (2013) 'Abandoned NHS IT system has cost £10bn so far', Guardian Online, 18 September. Available from: www.theguardian.com/society/2013/sep/18/nhs-records-system-10bn [Accessed 23 April 2017].

Final thoughts 08

So we come to the end of the conversation. A point at which theory needs to be replaced by action.

This is a book about how to *build and evolve our organizations people-first*, in a powerful way that everyone is a part of. It all comes back to people and I want to start this section by flipping the viewpoint for a moment and looking at it from their perspective. Because everything our workplaces do impacts people. Whoever they are, whatever their connection with the workplace may be, they feel that impact.

These are people with families, interests, ideas, capabilities. People with hopes, dreams, ambitions. They are people who, at school have been taught that their relationship with work should be a compromise – a transactional exchange of hours for money. As a result, we've reached a point where for many the relationship between themselves and work is nothing more than arbitrary numbness (just refer back to the Gallup employee engagement statistics from Chapter 1).

If that's the case in 87 per cent of relationships between worker and organization, not only do the businesses the majority of people work for miss out on the potential benefits that intense, connected contribution can bring, but the people themselves miss out. Spending much of your life unfulfilled or frustrated, overworked or stressed, has a knock-on impact on your family, your health, your community. It's a spiral of impact and not a good one.

Enabling people is the only requirement

Creating human workplaces where the number one commitment is to enable people to thrive, is the antidote to all of this and the starting point for an important new chapter in the relationship between people and organizations. Most importantly, it's eminently achievable and something we can all start working on now. Regardless of whether we sit at the top, bottom or middle of our organization, whether we're salaried, freelance or just loosely associated, if we connect with the purpose of a business, we can take responsibility and become a positive activist who helps drive it towards a positive new future.

That's an exciting opportunity!

A quick recap

Each human workplace creates its own definition. What it means to be people-first is determined by the combination of the business purpose, the behaviours it wants to drive, what it stands for and how it builds its organizational platform. Always with people in mind as its end users, the human workplace creates an experience that aims to have the right people, in the right places, doing the right things. It acknowledges that it's a constant work in progress, because things can always be improved and the world around it is constantly changing, but because of that acknowledgement it adopts cyclical design thinking that keeps it relevant.

Connecting people with the organization is essential, because the human workplace is a community that operates as a network. It's the successful unlocking of information to flow freely around the organization that creates this state, rather than the tearing down and restructuring of entire organizational structures. We've seen how some of the world's biggest brands are starting to humanize elements of their workplaces and we know that if they can do it, anyone can. Enhancing the connection between people by creating the right environments and driving the right actions that enable them to work at their absolute best, means the human workplace is a service provider to people. Making it real and becoming truly people-first can happen at any scale within an organization – it doesn't need to be a top-down, dictated clean sweep.

What it does need to be though, is authentic. Human workplaces are built on real connections and anything not done for the right reason will be recognized for what it is, because the power is with the crowd. In the community network, peer-to-peer sharing is open. News travels fast, but when harnessed to guide the organization, it will always be a force for progress.

We've explored tools and ideas for making this real and I hope they are useful. I've put them to good use in some amazing organizations and seen fantastic results, but as with anything, it's a question of adapting for context and situation. This book is a collection of ideas and tools, a starting point for perspectives that can be adapted and applied to your own organization.

Don't look on it as a *How to* guide, *The Human Workplace* is all about *What if ...*

And that's a fundamental point. Don't expect to have all the answers – it's OK not to know. Because finding out is where learning comes from. Today's right answer may be irrelevant tomorrow, so staying agile is the trick! The most human organization is the one that acknowledges its flaws, strives for improvement, enables its people and then gets out of the way so they can thrive.

Build: some final thoughts

These are some things that occurred to me in writing this book. You may find them useful extensions as you consider your own workplace.

The power of three

When looking at any aspect of your organization, always think in threes. Whether an idea, an action, or an option, it's better to work in multiples and three is the magic number.

- one is tokenistic;
- two is 50:50;
- three takes thought.

Any more (unless needed) takes too long.

Unlocking and unleashing

These words have been used a lot in this book, taking preference over the idea of creating a human workplace. That's because every organization already has all the elements in place to be more human.

It just needs to remove the barriers and allow the magic to happen!

The art of a great workplace

As I was nearing the end of writing this book, I was invited to speak at an event called *Open Sauce* in Bournemouth. With a Pecha Kucha slot on *Stop building companies, start building platforms* I turned the key ideas of the Human Workplace into a rap!

We covered the idea of seriousness early on in the book and it's that kind of rigidity and presumed rules around what we can and can't do that stop us from truly pushing the boundaries, experimenting and expressing ourselves. To be truly human (and reap the benefits of being so) our workplaces need to allow and encourage us to remove those shackles and embrace the art of our own work.

It's a leap of faith, but no truly great art ever emerged without an internal or external struggle of some kind.

Keeping an open mind

It's impossible to stay curious, adaptive and open to possibility if you come from a fixed mindset. For alternative perspectives and new ways of thinking to become viable, you need to be open to them. I always struggle when asked what I do, but I recently brought it down to the streamlined answer – *I turn up and see what happens.*

We all have the opportunity to do that in our work every day, but we have to be prepared to think on our feet and act in a way that responds to the world around us. It's dynamic and sometimes scary, but if we don't adopt this as our collective mindset, our organizations will continue doing what they've always done until that doesn't work anymore and they become irrelevant.

Just doing it

Alongside the ideas, the central message of this book is action. The only way to make anything happen, is by doing it.

Remember:

- There is no right or wrong way to create a human workplace, just the way that's right for yours.
- By starting small and using design thinking you can act for the right reasons and, if things don't go 100 per cent smoothly (they never do!), reiterate and keep making progress.
- The voice of the crowd in and around your organization is full of insight and feedback that can shape your actions. Listen to it.
- More than anything, keep moving forward. When you stop is when the world leaves you behind.

The last word

This is where I hand the baton to you. The ideas in *The Human Workplace* are those I've collected over the past few years of deep interaction with organizations of all shapes and sizes, as well as investigations into the relationships between people, work and the businesses they interact with. I've shared them with you in the hope that they might inspire you to unleash the humans in your organization, or become a positive activist that makes change in some small way. Every action creates impact and that's where potential comes from.

You don't have to arrive with the answers, it's fine to work them out as you go. Just turn up and see what happens!

Reference

The opening paragraphs of the conclusion were inspired by watching a short film:
Martinez Lara, D/Cano Mendez, R (2015) *Alike*. Available at: https://youtu.be/kQjtK32mGJQ [Accessed 23 April 2017].

INDEX